HOW TO LIVE
WITH YOUR
PARENTS
Without losing your mind!

by KEN DAVIS

A Book for Teenagers
That Every Parent Should Read.

GROW
FOR
IT!

ZONDERVAN™

GRAND RAPIDS, MICHIGAN 49530

ZONDERVAN™

How to Live with Your Parents Without Losing Your Mind
Copyright 1988 by Ken Davis

This is a Grow for It Book
Published by:
Zondervan, *Grand Rapids, Michigan 49530*

Library of Congress Cataloging in Publication Data

Davis, Ken, 1946-
    How to Live with your parents without losing your mind.

                    Summary: Advice for teenagers on how to get along with parents, drawing on
Christian precepts.
1. Teenagers—Religious life.   2. Family—Religioius Life—Juvenile literature.   3. Parent and
child—Juvenile literature. [1. Parent and child.   2. Conduct of life.   3. Christian life]   I. Title
BV4531.2.D37 1988   248.8'3   88-20685
ISBN 0-310-32331-2

Edited by David Lambert
Designed by the Church Art Works
Illustrated by Rand Kruback

Printed in the Unted States of America

04/DC/35 34

To the three women in my life:
Diane, Traci, and Taryn.
I love you.

Acknowledgments

I would like to express my gratitude to the following people for encouraging me and taking the time to critique my work. Many of their suggestions have been incorporated into this book.

Thank you, Keith Olson, for your valuable time and invaluable help.

Thank you, Kathy Colebank, for helping bring this material from chaos to coherency.

Thank you, Tim Swift, for believing in me enough to help make this book a reality.

Contents

Introduction

There are hundreds of books that advise parents on how to raise their children. But very few books have been written to help teenagers live with the people who read those books. This is one of the few.

"You're too idealistic," some people have told me. "Kids don't *care* about improving their relationship with their parents and they lack the interpersonal skills to accomplish it anyway." I disagree. I believe in you enough to think that you do care, and that you can make a difference in your home.

When my first child was born, I was ecstatic. My enthusiasm was immediately questioned by friends who said, "Wait until they hit the terrible twos – you'll wish you'd never had children." The terrible twos came and went, and they weren't that terrible.

"Wait until they enter grade school," well-meaning friends advised. "They'll turn into unrecognizable strangers." My children entered grade school, and in spite of some difficult adjustments, remained the same lovable friends I had always known.

But the best had been saved for last. "When they enter junior high," I was told, "it will be all over. You'll experience rebellion and mistrust and a breakdown in communication almost beyond your ability to bear." I approached that crossroad with dread. But now that my first child has reached her teens and has been in junior high for a year, I have yet to experience any of the catastrophes that were predicted. I must admit, though, that I've been reluctant to rejoice about that publicly. Invariably, when I do, someone will come up to tell me that judgment day is still coming.

Granted, each of these periods of my children's development has brought changes, and those changes have not always been easy for this dad to accept. There has been rebellion, backtalk, and more than one good fight in our home — but the predicted total breakdown in family relationships never occurred. And for that I can take no credit. It's partly due to the wonderful woman who claims that title of "mother" in our home, but I genuinely believe that most of the credit goes to unmerited blessing from God and to two children who, as individuals, have tried to demonstrate His love.

In fifteen years of working with youth, I have seen children from homes torn by conflict demonstrate that same love. On the other hand, I've seen teenagers from very loving homes make choices that brought extreme sorrow to their parents. Undoubtedly, it's because of that second group that so many adults have told me that you teenagers are not capable of the kind of love and wisdom it takes to live at peace with your family, and that to even suggest it would only make you feel guilty. I have more faith in your potential than that. Since the principles in this book were taken from the Bible, we can assume that God also felt you had great potential. At the very least, this book will give you some guidelines to shoot for.

As I struggle in the Christian life, I fail again and again — but each time, I look up to see the hand of my heavenly Father, waiting to help me on. And each time, the same Biblical guidelines that brought me that far are the guidelines I use to press onward. At the very best, this book will give you footholds and steppingstones from which you can make great progress toward living for Christ in your home.

As you read, if it seems that your family doesn't fit the pattern suggested in the book, please don't despair – the principles of love that Christ modeled for us do work. Whether you're from a single-parent family, a stepfamily, or one with both biological parents still present and accounted for, from a loving family or a family that is struggling to survive, you will find help here. This book is written for *you* because you are the key to change. God does not require you to be successful – He only requires that you be willing to try.

I refuse to expect my children to become the monsters that so many tell me they will become. Instead, I take the same view of them that I have of you. I believe that you have the potential to follow Christ and make changes in your life that will affect your family. So, in spite of the fact that adolescence brings with it some very difficult times, will you also refuse to accept the "inevitable" and, in the midst of the struggle, trust Christ to help you learn to live in love at home?

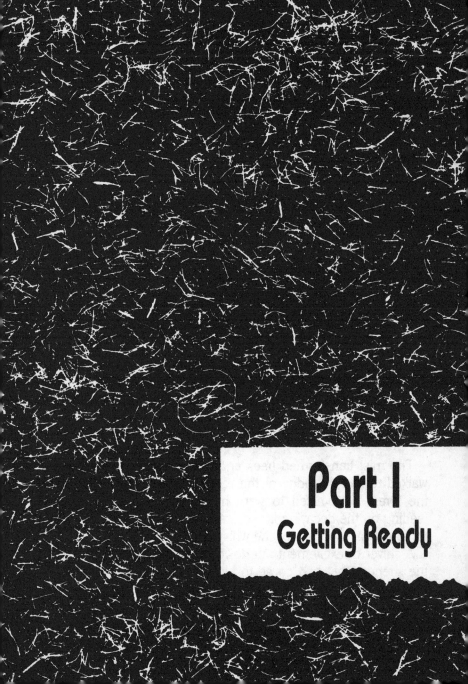

Part I
Getting Ready

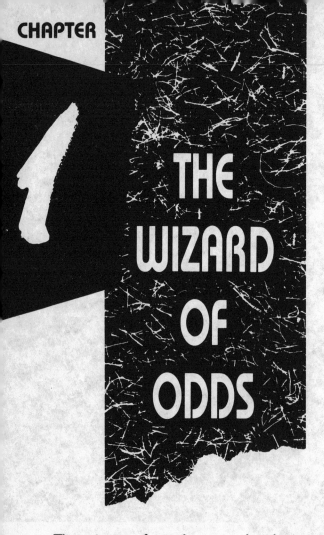

THE
WIZARD
OF
ODDS

The mist transformed trees and rocks into ghosts as the boy walked toward the edge of the meadow. Just before he entered the forest, he paused to warn his replacement of the jackals feeding on the decaying lion carcass nearby. "Be careful – they'll try to get the sheep, too," he whispered.

A shiver of excitement ran down his spine as he remembered the strength that had come to him when the lion had attacked. For a moment he had been afraid. But the fear had been overcome by a sudden surge of power, and seconds later the lion was dead. *Could not this same power be used against the enemies of my people?* he wondered as he moved through the mist-shrouded forest. Wasn't the power with him always? If it had just been the lion, he might have dismissed it as a fluke, or blind luck. But there had also been the bear. When he had felt the power surging through him, he had torn the bear apart with his own hands.

He moved faster through the dampness. The morning was bringing life to the forest and soon the sun would be up. Before long he would be with his brothers. He prayed they had not been killed in battle. Perhaps today he could save them. Today – perhaps – he would demonstrate the power against the enemy. How he had dreamed of tasting the bitterness of battle with his brothers by his side – but never had he been given the chance. Because he was too young, he had been left watching a few help- less animals on the side of a mountain. Sometimes he loathed his youth. It made him feel so helpless. Only the grown men had the power to change things. Only adult blood could be spilled to keep his people free.

Then, his father had granted him the privilege of bringing supplies to the front lines. For the past month, he had watched the enemy humiliate his nation's army, frightening them until they would not even fight. One terrible and powerful man had brought an entire army quivering to its knees. As a cat plays with a mouse, this man had taunted them. It was only a matter of time until his final pounce, and then all the boy's people would be sold into slavery. He did not know exactly what he would do, but today he would do something.

The supply pack bit into his shoulders as he approached the camp. The sun had not yet risen, and the damp air had taken on a lethal chill. All around him, soldiers were trying to prepare them- selves for war with the traditional battle cry – but the cry, stripped of its potency by the humiliating events of the past weeks, was now only a thin, reedy sound of cowardice.

The king had tried to boost morale by offering riches and the hand of his beautiful daughter to anyone who would kill this horrible foe, but no one had responded. The boy dropped his pack and fell in step with the soldiers. The evil one's blood-curdling shouts rumbled through the valley. Already his cursing and taunting was at a fever pitch. As they reached the top of a small ridge, even the meager battle cries around him died out, to be replaced by fearful whispers.

And then he saw him.

The departing mist added to his dimensions and diminished the ant-like men that accompanied him. Even at this distance he could see the hatred that burned in his huge, bloodshot eyes. He had seen that same evil stare in the eyes of the lion just before it attacked. Then their eyes met, and the boy felt the full power of blasphemous contempt. In dreamlike slow motion, the grotesque giant advanced, screaming his threats. The army had scattered in fear, and the boy stood alone, transfixed. He had been mocked by his own people. Even his brothers had accused him of being a conceited child, hungry to see blood spilled. *What strange power does this one man have?* the boy had asked. *The king has offered great wealth and favor to anyone who will kill the giant. Why hasn't someone tried to defeat him?* It wasn't his questions that were unacceptable. It was his age. A teenager had no right to ask such questions.

Suddenly the hills resounded with a screaming oath. The enemy was much closer now, enraged by this one who would dare to stand. The boy's feelings of fear and loneliness passed as quickly as they had come. Now he felt only the power, as he had felt it before when he had slain the bear and the lion. He knew that God would not forsake Him now. He bent and picked up five smooth stones from the creek bed.

As he advanced there was an audible gasp from the men behind him. This killer's armor weighed more than the boy's entire body. What could five little stones and a shepherd's sling do against such odds? What could a teenage boy do against this superhuman giant? When the evil warrior saw that his foe was a child, his face flushed with embarrassed rage, and he hurried in to kill him.

The soldiers watched in disbelief as the boy ran forward to meet certain death. On the run, he reached into his pouch, drew out one of the stones and slipped it into the sling. There was no doubt or fear now – the spell of the giant had been broken by the truth. The Lord God of Israel, who had helped him kill the bear and the lion, was now honoring his faith with the strength to overcome this impossible evil.

Hours of practice on the mountainside had made his movements automatic. The sling whistled in an arc above his head and, with a snap, whipped the stone to its mark. The giant was only a few paces away when it hit him. His huge legs collapsed midstride, and the momentum of his body carried him to the boy's feet. In his last few seconds of life the giant looked up into the clear eyes of the young boy. In that moment he too became aware of the power – the power of a living and mighty God, brought by faith to its fullest potential in the life of a teenage boy named David. But for Goliath, the realization came too late. (Taken from I Samuel 17.)

What does the story of David and Goliath have to do with you and your parents? It's simple – you can use the lessons learned from David's faith to live in peace with your family.

But before you run outside to find five smooth stones to throw at your mother and father, take a look at the next few pages. I want to help you see that the same God that helped David overcome impossible odds can also help you. There are, in fact, amazing parallels between this story and the situations you face in your family. Certain steps that David took in defeating Goliath you, too, can use to face the problems in your family. For one thing, David knew how big the giant was. That's important. Then he recognized that something had to be done, and that God had chosen *him* to do it. Finally, he simply trusted God – and did it.

Let's take a look at how those steps can help you make a difference in your family.

KNOW HOW BIG THE GIANT IS

Finding a solution to the family problems you face may seem about as possible as fighting a giant ten times your size. Most kids I've counseled over the past twenty years have had little hope that their problems could ever be resolved – so they've given up on their families. One young man said to me, "You know, my parents never even talk to me unless I'm in trouble or they want me to do something."

After I presented an assembly program on self-worth, a sixteen-year-old girl approached me. "I would like to think that I'm worthwhile," she said, "but I'm not sure. My friends say I am, but – " and before she could continue she began to cry. I stood silently while she wept. When she regained her composure, she continued: "I wish my mom felt I was worthwhile." Again she cried, and between sobs she told me that she had recently been admitted to a hospital. The doctors notified her mother that the situation could be serious. But her mother refused to come to the hospital – after all, she had an important date. The message to my young friend was loud and clear: *Even if your life is threatened, my plans are more important than you.* How hopeless she must have felt.

Many teenagers want to spend as little time in the house as possible. For them, home is not a pleasant place to be. Some feel that their parents don't understand them – and some are right. Forty percent of teenagers in a recent survey said they felt their parents didn't care about the problems they face in everyday life.

When you read these stories and statistics, and when you consider the everyday problems you face in your own family, the situation looks bleak. And in many ways it is. *Making a difference in your family is not going to be easy.* The odds are enormous. Just like David, you are facing a giant. But it's even more important to realize that *the task is not impossible.* Don't make the giant

 The Wizard of Odds

bigger than he is. I'm sure there were some men in King Saul's army who had never actually *seen* Goliath. When they heard him yell, they ran without even stopping to look. They beat it to the rear of the battle lines, telling everyone that Goliath was bigger than a building and smoked camels. Not Camel cigarettes – real live camels. And we do the same thing. Maybe you've heard from friends that parents don't give a rip. Maybe you've decided to give up because the odds against your parents ever learning to get along with you are just too great. Well, I have good news for you. I have seen the giant – and he just ain't that big.

I've counseled with hundreds of teenagers concerning family problems. They all felt their problems were unsolvable. Later, they discovered that God was big enough to help them – but at first they thought it was hopeless. Maybe you're thinking:

> My problem is impossible.
> My parents are incapable of change.
> The odds are too great.
> My sin can never be forgiven.

Does your family have problems? You can have the strength to face those problems, but only if you can manage to believe one simple fact:

> **No matter how impossible your situation, God has the power to help you overcome it.**

The apostle Paul, who faced overwhelming odds much of his life, said: "I can do everything through him who gives me strength" (Philippians 4:13). So Paul faced a few problems – things like shipwreck, jail cells, beatings, poisonous snakebites, blindness, and many others. So what? He saw no reason to give up. He had great connections. He personally knew the one who had overcome death itself. Paul believed there was nothing too big for God.

If you're a Christian, *you* have the same connections. God specializes in impossibilities. Once Jesus said to the disciples, "It is easier to get a camel through the eye of a needle than to get a rich man into heaven" (Matthew 19:24). What would *you* have said to that if you'd been one of the disciples? You'd have thought, *Even if you could get a camel through the eye of a needle, you would have one terribly strung-out camel.* "If this is true then no one can go to heaven," they said. But Jesus put the whole thing in perspective when He said, "With man this is impossible, but with God all things are possible."

Learning to really show the love of Christ in your home *will* at times seem impossible – but you're not without God's help. The lion wasn't big enough to defeat the team of God and David. Goliath was big enough to intimidate a whole army, but he was no match for God and the faith of a teenage boy. Your situation is not too big for God and you to handle. It is okay to be afraid because you realize that the odds are great, but please also recognize that your God is greater. He is the wizard of odds, and you and He together are unbeatable.

RECOGNIZE THAT SOMETHING MUST BE DONE

I hope that you aren't satisfied with the status quo in your home. I hope that, even though you don't know exactly what to do yet, you're ready and willing to do something. Unfortunately, many teenagers resign themselves to ride out family difficulties until they leave home. They decide to ignore the problems until they no longer have to face them. If that was a viable solution, this book would end right here. But ignoring family problems is not a solution. At best, it's only a postponement. If the problems you face at home aren't dealt with now, you'll be dismayed to discover they will follow you when you leave home. They will follow you to your job, to your marriage, and to virtually every other kind of relationship too. Correctional officials know this is true. Most of the men and women in prison never learned to live at home. They couldn't deal with their parents' authority; they could hardly wait to get away from their parents. They refused to face their problems, and as a result the problems followed them.

David could have chosen to ignore the problem of Goliath, but Goliath wouldn't have gone away. The Philistines would have conquered the country and David would have lived in slavery the rest of his life. He used God's strength to face the problem, and he saved his country as well as himself.

Every family has room for improvement. Those who say, "There are no problems in my family" often find that there were problems, all right – they were just blind to them. Yes, your family may be better than most. But don't pass up the opportunity to make it better yet. It doesn't matter that most of your friends are unwilling to try to make a difference in their families. Nor does it matter that the odds are against you. Like David, you can choose to be a giant killer. You can choose to step out from the crowd. That choice will lead to a challenge like you have never faced before. It will initiate an adventure that will affect you for the rest of your life.

And remember this: If you have committed your life to Christ and wish to follow His leading, there is no other option. The fifth commandment is, "Honor your father and your mother" (Exodus 20:12). Scripture insists that you honor and obey your parents. In Romans 1:30, those who disobey their parents are included in the same list with God-haters and murderers. Not exactly a "most likely to succeed" list. God makes it clear that an unwillingness to demonstrate His love in the home is a sign of rebellion against Him. He also makes it clear that your efforts to honor your parents will be rewarded by a wonderful change in your life.

In addition, you will increase the chances of establishing a good home for your own children. My mother used to say, "You will be able to tell how your wife will treat you by watching the way she treats her father." She was right. You will carry into your marriage the same basic attitudes and behavior patterns you demonstrated toward your parents. Maybe that's why God insisted that we take steps to live in harmony with our parents.

Here are a few examples of how important this is to God. "Children, obey your parents in the Lord, for this is right. 'Honor your father and mother' – which is the first commandment with a promise – 'that it may go well with you and that you may enjoy long life on the earth'" (Ephesians 6:1-3). You see? According to the Bible your efforts may even help you live longer. Colossians

3:20 says, "Obey your parents in everything, for this pleases the Lord." If obeying your parents pleases the Lord, get a load of how cursing your parents affects Him. In five different places (Exodus 21:17, Leviticus 20:9, Proverbs 20:20, Matthew 15:4, and Mark 7:10), God said that anyone who curses his father or mother must be put to death.

Do you get the feeling He is not too pleased with those who write their parents off? I wasn't kidding about the fact there are no options, and it's obvious that God isn't kidding either. It is right, it is wise, it is important, and it is healthy to learn to love your parents. In John 13, Christ told His disciples that people would know they were His followers if they loved each other with the same kind of love He had demonstrated toward them. There is nothing that reflects your commitment to Christ more clearly than that love. I can listen to your testimony and not know the level of your commitment. I can hear you sing beautiful songs and see your involvement in the church and still not know the level of your commitment. But let me watch you with your mother and father for an hour and I will have a good idea of how serious you are about your faith. If you refuse to love your family, then I can legitimately question the depth of your love for Christ. 1 John 4:20 says, "If anyone says, 'I love God,' yet hates his brother, he is a liar."

Let's be realistic. If there are serious problems between you and your parents now, you shouldn't expect to develop a healthy attitude toward them overnight. It can take years to really become consistent in this kind of love. But unless you start now, it will *never* happen. Very few of the commands that Jesus gave us are easy to follow, and this one is especially difficult. But that doesn't excuse us from the responsibility to work toward the goals He has set before us.

When Jesus sent out the disciples He told them to be witnesses first in Jerusalem, then in Judea, and finally in the uttermost parts of the earth. In other words, He wanted them to start where they lived. You live at home.

If you're aware of problems in that home, then something needs to be done – not just because you want to see those problems resolved, but also because God has commanded it. He wants your attitude (honor your parents) and your actions (obey your parents) to be in line with His Word. You are the only one who can make the change. It's up to you. The rest of the army has fled. What are you going to do? If you are willing to change, the rest of this book will help to show you how.

GOD HAS CHOSEN YOU TO MAKE A DIFFERENCE IN YOUR HOME

One of the most common actions taken by teenagers concerned about family problems is to pray that God will change their parents. That's okay, but it does not relieve you of your responsibility. Imagine David quickly kneeling as the giant approached and praying, "Please God – shrink him! Shrink him!" God chose David even though he seemed the least likely person for the job. He has chosen you, even though you have the least power and the least to say about what changes can or can't be made. God does not choose on the basis of power, beauty, talent, intelligence, or age. He chooses those who are willing to trust and obey Him. The fact that you are concerned enough to read this far may make you the only candidate for this challenge.

Although you don't have the power to insist on changes in your family, you do have the power to change the most important thing of all. *You!*

That's why this book is written to you. It's not written to give you hints on how to change your parents. The change must start with you. I will suggest some practical places to start. But first let me demonstrate how important it is to start with you. Get some paper and make a list of all the things that are wrong with the other members of your family. Put each family member's name at the top of a piece of paper. Then list all the ways they need to change. If your father yells too much, include that in the list. If you have a brother or sister who needs to be locked in a padded room, write it down. Take your time and write down every bad thing you can think of. Don't turn this page until you have thought of everything. Don't leave anything out. When you are finished and totally steamed up about how wrong everybody is, then and only then you may turn this page.

DON'T CHEAT!

I ASKED YOU TO WRITE DOWN *ALL* YOUR COMPLAINTS BEFORE YOU TURNED THE PAGE.

It will be worth it to get this off your chest. Now go back and make a complete list.

Now that you have pin-pointed the faults of your family, you may be interested to know this:

THERE IS NOTHING YOU CAN DO TO CHANGE ONE TINY THING YOU HAVE WRITTEN.

You can't change other people. One of the first steps you need to take to build new relationships with your family is to throw away the list you just made. Better yet, burn it – and as it burns, admit to yourself and to God that there isn't anything you can do about any of the things on that list. Thinking about those things will only get in the way of making the changes you do have the power to make.

Now, on another piece of paper, write down all the things about yourself that need to change. Maybe you get mad too easily or don't help around the house as much as you should. Maybe you lie or deceive your parents. List everything you can think of.

Have you thought of everything?

With Christ, you have the power to change everything you have just written. And that's where the great potential is for you to effect a change in your whole family. You are a big part of what makes your family a family. Even if you're the only one to change, your family will have changed. If you insist on blaming others for the problems and keep waiting for them to change, nothing will improve. You'll be expecting results in an area over which you have no control. The July 1987 issue of *Readers Digest* contained the story of a young girl whose parents were unbelievably cold and heartless. Her situation seemed so hopeless that she tried to take her own life. Fortunately she failed – and lived to become a healthy young adult who loved life. Years later, she looked back and made an observation that contains the secret to *your* success, as well as hers: "My school counselor suggested I seek professional help. I told her it wouldn't do any good since I knew the situation at home and school would never change. Of course I was overlooking one critical, life-saving fact – that *it was possible for me to change* ... I am so changed that it seems like a millennium since that March night six years ago."

David faced the same problem as that girl and as you – he had no power or rank. God did not ask him to change the army or the giant or his brothers. God changed David. All of the frustrations of being "just a kid" are not enough to keep God from using you. If you will let Him, He will give you the power to make the changes in your life that need to be made.

YOU MUST TRUST GOD

If you are willing to trust God, you will find Him to be faithful.

That discovery will change not just your family situation but your whole life – whether you are facing the odds of defeating a giant, overcoming a drug dependency, dealing with an impossible home situation, or trying to find a reason for living. God is a specialist at impossible odds. He conquered the greatest odds of all when He sent His Son to die for you. When you, in faith, trust in Christ for the forgiveness of your sins, He not only is faithful in forgiving your sins, but He gives you the power to face impossible odds every day. He is the wizard of odds. Without Him you are like a lost, helpless sheep unable to face a giant – or even a dwarf. If that sounds like you, you can change that right now. If you have never done so, why not ask Christ to forgive you of your sins. Give yourself to Him, and allow Him to make you the kind of person you were created to be. He has the power to do what you cannot do. He can change you from a "lost sheep" to a *super sheep,* from a defeated kid to a Child of God. You will discover that He can be trusted in every area of your life. If you have already trusted Him with your life, then take a moment right now to recommit your life to Him. The way we demonstrate our trust in God is by simple obedience. Are you willing to obey Him as the Holy Spirit directs? If so, get ready. You will come face to face with the power of a living God. Not just to read about or hear about, but to experience first hand in your life.

INSIDE A PARENT'S HEAD

Is there a computer chip inside a parent's head programed to ruin your life? What's in there that gets them so bent out of shape and makes them say "no" so much of the time? Is there anything inside their heads at all?

This chapter is designed to help you answer some of those questions. It will help you understand how a parent thinks and what makes those unreasonable, unyielding, weird people called parents act the way they do.

If you are between the ages of eleven and eighteen, your mind is probably already made up. You believe that when your parents' feet touch the floor in the morning, the first thought that crosses their minds is, "How can I make them suffer today?"

Nothing could be further from the truth. Sure, some of the things that have happened in your family and some of the things you've seen on TV shows can lead you to believe that parents and teenagers are warring factions bent on destroying one another. Parents are often portrayed in film and music as mean, cruel, or stupid. If you believe that, you can expect trouble. But your parents are not your enemy. Understanding that is the first step toward discovering what is inside your parent's head. If you insist on believing that your parents exist to make your life miserable, it will be impossible for you to live at peace with them. But – believe me – I know it isn't always easy to shake that belief.

Some of our first conscious experiences back in babyhood make it seem as though Mom and Dad's main responsibility is to keep us from having fun. One of my first memories was of having my hand slapped for trying to stick a fingernail file into an electrical outlet. Why would these cruel giants resort to physical punishment just to keep me from experiencing the joy of putting this object into the hole it was obviously made to fit? At the time, it seemed like they were simply trying to destroy my fun. I had never enjoyed the thrill of 110 volts coursing through my tiny body. Why would they deny me such an experience?

A few days ago I celebrated my fortieth birthday. On several occasions in those forty years I have experienced the thrill of 110 volts coursing through my body (which is no longer tiny). It was never done on purpose and once it almost cost me my life. Now I know why my hand was slapped. So, when my own daughter discovered an electrical outlet and tried to jam a butter knife into it,

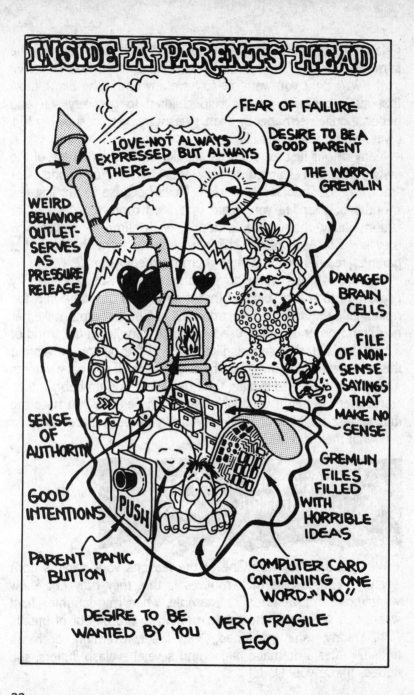

I slapped her hand and said, "No!" She looked at me with the same look I gave my parents. It was a wide-eyed hurt look that said, "Why don't you want me to have any fun?" She didn't know that such behavior causes little children to get very stiff and become quite permanently dead. I wasn't trying to destroy her fun, I was trying to save her life.

Many of our first experiences are like this incident. One of the first words you learned to say was "NO!" Not "daddy" or "mommy" or "cookie," but "No!" That's because in the first few months of your life you heard that word more than any other. Unfortunately, many parents don't take the time to explain why they say no. As a result, children begin to form the idea that parents are enemies that keep them from enjoying life.

There are times when an explanation just isn't possible. Try explaining to a two year old that if she sticks the knife into the outlet, little things called electrons will run up her arm, make her hair stand on end, and cause her toes to smoke. In the world of a two year old, that sounds like fun, and the person preventing this experience is nothing less than a monster. If you have parents who take the time to explain their decisions, you probably understand them better. If you don't have such parents, you have the difficult responsibility of looking behind your parents' decisions to see what their motivations really are.

INSIDE A PARENT'S HEAD IS AN AUTOMATIC "NO" REFLEX

Why do they say no? One of the reasons your parents don't always communicate their motives is that *they may not know what those motives are.* For example, when my daughter Traci was seven years old, she came running to me all out of breath. "Oh, Daddy," she exclaimed, "can I stay overnight at Kim's house?" After a dramatic pause and several eyelash flutters, she added, "I love you, Dad."

My response was immediate. "No," I said. Not unkindly, but with a finality that indicated I meant it. It was a short word, I could spell it, and it didn't require any thinking.

"Okay," Traci responded sadly.

My wife Diane, who had observed this whole encounter, chose this moment to gently prod me. "Why did you say no?" she asked.

I responded as any intelligent and reasonably mature father would respond. "Just because I said no!" I snapped. What I really meant was, "I don't know why I said no and I don't want to have to expend the energy it will take to figure out why I said no." I felt my authority was being questioned. However, Diane has a way of pressing until she gets an answer. And the more she pressed, the more I was surprised to discover that I really didn't know why I had said no. Diane pointed out that Traci had been very good, the home she wanted to visit was a nice home with trustworthy parents, and Kim was a very well-behaved and enjoyable friend.

I suddenly realized that my decision was not just out of habit – I also had a reason. I was still trying to protect Traci. Just like me, sometimes your parents say no because that's the word they have used to save your life since the day you were born. Now they are using it automatically and don't even know why. I was there when Traci struggled to be born. I lay awake many nights after she was born listening to make sure she was breathing. When she was one year old I watched her fall down a flight of stairs. When she was two I rode to the hospital with her because she had poured boiling water all over her legs. It seems like just last week that only a constant vigil on my part kept her from killing herself. It seems like only yesterday that she wouldn't even leave the room unless I went with her. Now today she wanted to go over to Kim's house. *Alone!* In many ways I want her to still need me. She is thirteen years old and I still feel like she isn't safe without me. I will always feel this way. I also realize that soon there will be a boy hanging around our door and I'll probably want to shoot him. He will want to take my daughter on some dangerous and temptation-filled adventure called a date, and he won't want me to come along. It will be very hard not to say *no*.

When I understood that my negative response to Traci's request was born out of an undue concern for her safety and an exaggerated idea of my role as her protector, I also realized that it was unfair. I was wrong to not allow her this privilege, so I changed my mind. But my motives had never been wrong. If it hadn't been for the probing of my wife, I might never have understood why I said no.

When your mom and dad brought you home it seemed as though you were programed to self destruct. They were programed to keep you from self destruction. Small babies look for trouble from birth. They eat marbles, silver polish, cleaning fluid, and any other dangerous items they can find. They seek out highways, high stools, and high-voltage wires rather than the harmless toys parents provide for them. The point is this: Even when your parents are wrong, most of the time their motives are right. That may not seem like much consolation if your parents have just kept you from attending your favorite party, but knowing that they do act out of love can make a big difference in the way you respond.

Here's another fact that may surprise you. Sometimes parents say no just because they like to have you around. I love to have my children near me; there are times I don't want my girls to go anywhere just so they will be with me. But as they grow older, school activities, church functions, friends, and a million other interests will pull them away from home. That's what's happening in your family right now. Unfortunately, parents don't often plan anything more exciting than watching TV. When you could be with your friends, you end up trapped at home. Try to remember, when that happens, that your mom and dad need to have you around at least enough to feel that you are an important part of their lives. It may seem weird, but that's part of what is inside a parent's head. Your parents may even resent your friends and your activities because those things take you away. Those things remind them that before too long, you will no longer need them. Parents have feelings just like you. They need to feel needed. Much of their self-worth depends on being needed by *you*. Then, just about the

Inside a Parent's Head

time you get old enough to share experiences with, just about the time you develop the maturity and intellectual capacity to be an enjoyable companion, you begin choosing other companions to spend your time with. Yes, it's natural for this to happen – but it can be a very hard time for your mom and dad.

Most parents enjoy getting away from the kids once in a while. And, unfortunately, there are a few parents who do not seem to enjoy the company of their children at all. If that sounds like your parents, it may be that they are just busy or preoccupied. Although living with that attitude can be hard on your self-esteem, it doesn't mean that your parents don't love you. In my case, I can only take separation from my kids for a short period of time. Our house without the fighting, laughing, and racket of children is like a ghost town. It rings hollow and lonesome and I don't like it. Parents act like they can't live with you, but in truth they can't live without you. Your parents want to be a part of your life, and they want you to be a part of theirs. Inside that head they know they are losing you, and the word *no* can become a weapon. Not against you, but against the forces that take you away.

There is also a little monster in a parent's head that causes them to say no. This monster is called a "sense of authority." Demonstrating authority has a tendency to make a parent feel in control. And that authority is never threatened more than when a child begins to make decisions on his or her own. One mother told me that after her child has been granted several privileges in a row, she says no just to prove she still has the authority. I have a tendency to do the same – to say no once in a while just to prove I'm still the boss. And if I'm challenged to defend myself, watch out! It's like pouring salt in an open wound. Parents fear losing control; saying no is a way *to feel in control.* Is that wrong? I believe it is – but *the motive behind it is not.* This is a special weakness of many parents. There are ways to reassure your mom and dad that they are still in control so they won't have to say no just to prove it. These are discussed in chapter 7.

The role of a parent naturally lends itself to criticism. The price of raising a child in love is that you will sometimes be hated for that love. That makes sense, if you think about it. After all, parents who don't love, don't set guidelines. They never say no.

When I was working with boys who were in trouble with the law I saw a perfect example of this. I was employed with Youth for Christ as a guide in the wilderness canoeing area of northern Minnesota. Each week I took boys on a rugged wilderness canoe trip. Many of these boys were referred to us by the juvenile division of the police department. One of the most troubled boys I ever met went with us three weeks in a row. It's tragic to see a twelve-year-old boy who already has a criminal record. But even more tragic was the lack of joy in this boy's life. There was no laughter, no pride, no self-respect. This boy hated himself and everyone around him. His name was Billy.

When Billy asked to go with us a fourth week, I began to wonder about the parent permission slips he brought each week. I checked with his mother and found out he had forged the permission slips. I also found the root of his problem. Billy had no father, and his mother had not even known where he was for those three weeks. Even worse, she didn't really care. To her, Billy was only a nuisance. She told me that, during his absence, she had thought he might be at his grandmother's house. But in three weeks she had never bothered to check. When I apologized for not checking more carefully, she said, "It doesn't matter. I would've signed the permission slips just to get him out of the house." All of this was said with Billy standing right there.

When I had Billy alone, I asked, "If your mom would have let you go anyway, why did you forge the permission slips?"

It was the only time I saw him soften. Looking at the ground, he said, "I wanted you to think I had someone who cared." Billy would've loved to have someone care enough to say no. If your parents make decisions that go against your desires and occasionally say no, take heart. It's a sign that they care.

INSIDE A PARENT'S HEAD THERE LIVES A GREMLIN

The worry gremlins that live in your parents' heads cause them to think the very worst when it comes to your welfare. If you are thirty minutes late getting home, the gremlin goes to the file he keeps in a corner of their heads. In this file he stores all of the worst catastrophes you can possibly think of. He brings them to your mom and dad's minds one at a time every time you are late, every time you give your parents reason to worry. That's why they always think the worst has happened:

You've been hurt in a car accident.
You've been kidnapped by perverts.
Aliens are using your body for scientific experiments.
**You've run away to Los Angeles to sell yourself
on the street.**

It doesn't matter that you may not be able to get to Los Angeles in thirty minutes from where you live. The gremlin doesn't have to present reasonable ideas. They only have to be horrible.

When Traci left recently for a school outing in the mountains, I lay awake the whole first night fighting the gremlins. Would she die freezing in a snowbank? Would a freak avalanche crush her little body? Would a teacher go mad and shoot everyone? I even thought about the legendary "big-foot" dragging her off to feed his family. As a Christian parent I know that I'm supposed to trust my children to the care of a loving Father. I should think of all of the good experiences she will have and be happy. But the gremlin makes it very hard not to worry. Because of him, it was hard to consent to her going in the first place.

The gremlin lives! Knowing he is in there may help you understand why your parents are so paranoid sometimes. The next time you are tempted to tell one of your parents not to make a federal case out of it when you're thirty minutes late, remember the gremlin.

INSIDE A PARENT'S HEAD
THERE IS MORE THAN EMPTY SPACE

While writing this chapter, I told a teenage friend the title was "Inside a Parent's Head." He asked if I was going to list all the things inside a parent's head. When I said yes, he laughed. "Short chapter, huh?" he said, as he turned and walked away.

It will be hard to get along with your parents if you believe that between those two ears is only empty space. You may think that's why so much of what you say goes in one ear and out the other – there is nothing there to stop it. I have heard the word *stupid* used more than once when listening to a teenager describe his or her parents. But your parents are not stupid! Will Rogers, a twentieth-century American humorist, said that as a teenager he could not believe how ignorant his father was. But by the time he turned twenty-one, he couldn't believe how much his father had learned in such a short period of time. Because you may fail to understand their motives and because parents act rather strangely at times, it's easy to conclude that they're a few bricks short of a full load. Hold onto that belief, and you'll make it difficult or impossible to improve relationships in your home.

I admit that parents are a little weird. But some of the greatest geniuses in history were a little weird.

Bill Cosby has a hilarious routine where he presents evidence that all children have brain damage. His premise is that, no matter what question they are asked, kids always respond with "I dunno." He may be right – but I think it's safe to say that the damage we suffer as parents is even more severe. We say things that make no sense. Parents shout things like, "If you cut your legs off playing around with that lawnmower, don't you come running to me!" Even little kids know you can't run without legs.

The other day, I found myself asking my daughter Taryn a question I didn't even want her to answer. I looked her directly in the eye and asked, "Do you think I'm stupid?" How was she supposed

to answer? She said nothing, but the question itself was not exactly intelligent.

Not long ago I heard a parent demand, "Look at me when I'm talking to you," followed immediately by "Don't you look at me like that!" No wonder the evidence seems to lead to the conclusion that we aren't too sharp.

But before you begin nodding and whispering under your breath, "I told you so," consider this: *you caused the damage!* When you were born your father had all of his mental capacities. He leaned over your crib and with emotion and pride said, "I'm so proud." You responded by looking cross-eyed, slobbering, throwing up, and making a dirty diaper. At that moment, brain cells started to die. And from that moment, your dad would never be the same.

When I was first married I was a relatively bright young man. I held a 3.5 average in college and could think clearly. I spent the first three months of fatherhood without sleep, listening for my child to breathe. I spent the next ten years trying to keep two children from killing themselves and each other. One day I walked into the living room to see my one-year-old standing at the top of the stairs leading to the basement. She had never stood up in her life. Now here she stood at the top of the stairs wobbling like a drunken sailor. Why did she pick this spot? What goes through a child's mind? Is she thinking, "This will freak my daddy out!" In panic I yelled her name, "Traci!" I frightened her and she fell down the stupid stairs. Fortunately, God makes little children out of rubber. She sustained no damage. But I did!

Of course, I'm being facetious. I don't have actual brain damage, and neither do your parents. But we *have* become accustomed to responding to situations by saying things that don't make a lot of sense. You can take comfort in the fact that this disease does not affect just your parents. It affects all parents. I know you won't take any comfort in this next fact, but listen anyway: The disease is hereditary and someday you will have it too.

As I grew up I saw a particular expression common to angry

Inside a Parent's Head

parents used dozens of times. It was meaningless and incredibly useless. Most of you will recognize this procedure as soon as I begin to describe it. In this ritual the angry parent places his hand at about eyebrow level, like a military salute, and says, "I have had it with you clear up to here!" They usually continue making little salute movements as they speak.

I always wanted to ask, "What have you had?" But I also wanted to live, so I didn't. I also wondered what was so special about that eyebrow area. I never saw a parent make that gesture at waist level or below the knee. They had always had it up to that good old eyebrow spot. As much as I loathed this expression, about five years ago, I found myself using it. (Don't laugh – you will too.) When I finished, my daughter, pointing toward the space between my eyebrow and the top of my head, said, "Well, Dad, you've got about that much left."

The point? Admit that your parents are a little strange and allow them that. Part of that strangeness was brought about by loving and raising you.

Most parents want to be good parents. They don't want to fail. They want to provide a good home, and they feel guilty when things go wrong. *Talk* to them about some of the ideas discussed in this chapter. Choose a good time – a quiet time when there are no conflicts. Use this book as a springboard for discussion. Let them know that you love them and that you realize the job of being a parent isn't easy. But don't even bother opening the discussion if you're just doing this to get something that you want – like a new car or permission for a weekend trip. You'll be dead before you start.

These questions might give you a good opening:

Mom, I was reading this GREAT book by Ken Davis that says sometimes parents say no just because they like to have their kids around. Do you ever feel that way?

When I question a decision you make, does that make you angry? Why?

Ken Davis, the handsome, talented author I'm reading, says that sometimes he worries so much about bad things happening to his kids that he doesn't let them go places. Why do parents worry so much? Do you worry about me?

How can I get ready to be a good parent?

You can probably think of even better questions. Ask them – and then listen carefully to the answers your parents give you. Beneath what they say, you will hear them telling you the kind of parent they would like to be. Put aside some of your pride and misconceptions and look carefully at your mother and father. You will see that your parents do care. Even when they are wrong, most of the time their motives are right. Walk in their shoes this week. Feel some of the pressures they feel. Then ask God for the courage and strength to touch them with love. I think you will discover that what's inside a parent's head is a whole lot of love.

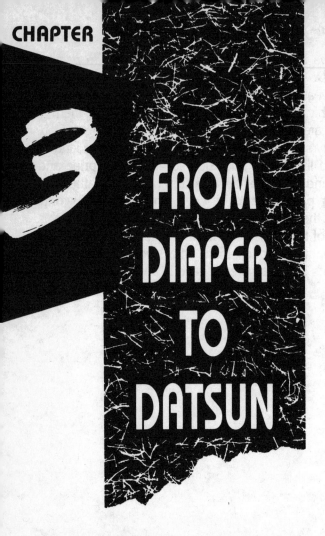

FROM DIAPER TO DATSUN

Knowing the forces that shaped your family can help you understand your parents. Once you understand the reasons for their behaviors and attitudes it is easier to be tolerant of their actions. Before you were even a gleam in your father's eye, (I got that saying from my dad) events had been working to shape how your family operates. When you were born you became one of those events. Your unique personality brought changes that would not have happened if you had not come along. The specific needs of your parents and brothers and sisters have also had a profound influence on your family. This chapter will help you discover what those influences are.

PREHISTORIC LIFE (BEFORE YOU WERE BORN)

Before you were born, the attitudes and actions of the people around your parents began to shape the situation you live in right now. Things that happened before you decided to "drop in" have affected how your parents respond to you now.

One of those influences is the traditions your parents grew up with. Maybe your parents grew up with traditions that have been handed down for generations; for instance, that special family get-together that you so despise could be much more important than you realize. You'll be affected by those traditions either way — whether your parents choose to continue them or rebel against them.

So take the time to discover your heritage; it's worth it. I'm not suggesting that you spend hours roaming through graveyards or sitting in libraries doing research. A few good questions to your parents, grandparents, and aunts and uncles should tell you what you need to know. And it's important to remember that knowing this information doesn't make you a prisoner of your past. If you discover that Uncle Harry died when a platform on which he was standing collapsed at a public gathering (in other words, he was hanged for stealing chickens), you are not destined to lead a life of crime.

If your family's ethnic or religious origin is different from those around you, that may tell you the secret of why your parents respond differently than the parents of your friends.

If you had an older brother or sister who was very good in athletics, your parents may expect the same of you. You may already be experiencing the pain of being expected to live up to the reputation of someone else. On the other hand, if you had an

From Diaper to Datsun

older brother or sister who was in trouble with the law or involved with drugs, your parents may be overprotective with you. If so, you probably hate that – but remember that the pain your parents experience on behalf of your brother or sister is intense, almost unbearable. They aren't trying to punish you for someone else's mistakes. They are trying to protect you (and themselves) from going through all that pain again. Similarly, when parents have lost a child or had a difficult time having a baby, they will often be overprotective of the next children to come along. And some parents feel that they've failed with one of their children and try to make it up raising the next one.

Your parents are also affected by how their parents treated them. If your parents' mother and father were very strict, they could respond in one of two ways. In an effort to spare you some of the pain they encountered as teenagers, they could be much more lenient with you than their parents were. But it's more likely that they will treat you like their parents did, because it is the only example they had.

There is, after all, no school for being a parent. You aren't one until you are one. Most parents rely greatly on how *their* parents raised *them* as the example for how to raise their own children – and that's true whether their parents were good parents or poor parents. I know (because I did it too) that many of you are right this moment vowing that you will *never* respond to your children as your parents do to you. You will be much more understanding, loving, and lenient. But, regardless of your intentions, you'll make a lot of the same mistakes your parents do. We tend to follow the patterns and habits of our parents whether those patterns were good or bad. Statistics show that children who are abused often become abusive parents. Many children raised in alcoholic homes struggle with alcoholism in their own lives. On the positive side, children who are raised in a loving and understanding atmosphere tend to develop the same environment for their own children.

That's why I believe the information in this book is so important. Christ *can* give you the power to reverse a negative pattern. If you look carefully at how your parents were raised, you may understand more clearly why they act the way they do. You may also see clearly how you can break a chain of problems and become the catalyst for positive change in your home. When you don't know the reason for your parents' actions, you'll tend to respond in anger. The problem remains unresolved – and later, when you marry, that same problem will probably be carried into your own family. If you see your parents as the enemy, when you become a parent you will assume the role of enemy. Knowing what has caused your parents to behave the way they do equips you to love and understand them. Your future family will directly benefit from the efforts you expend today.

Discovering this information about your family background can often be fun as well as enlightening. Parents like thinking back to the good old days. At the end of this chapter, I've suggested some questions to get things started. Don't be surprised if your parents get carried away answering these questions. Don't even ask unless you are prepared to listen with interest. Even though you may have to hear about how your mom and dad had to walk to school twenty miles in the snow, ill-clad, with no shoes, uphill both ways, with Indians attacking every fifty feet, if you listen carefully you will also hear clues about how they became what they are today. Listen with compassion, and you may even gain a new respect for your mom and dad.

You'll be surprised, for instance, to find out that your folks had feelings just like you. If you ask your mom how she met your dad, you may discover that they kissed and steamed up some car windows while looking at the moon. (I know that even the thought of this probably makes you want to throw up. But resist the urge and read on.)

THEN CAME YOU

All of the above is prehistoric – it happened before you were born. Then the world got lucky. Then came you.

Whether you're the first child or the fourteenth, no one really

knew how to deal with you until you were here. God made you with special gifts and physical attributes that no one else on the face of the planet has – and those unique qualities affect how you are treated as a teenager.

My first baby, Traci, was even-tempered and mild from the day she was born. She was almost like an angel. She told us what her name was and then proceeded to eat anything we gave her. She did her diaper thing right on schedule, gently told us she would appreciate having it changed, and slept all night. Taryn, our second child, came out screaming. She let us know that she was in charge and was furious that somewhere along the way she had lost her luggage. Interestingly, I think it was the second child, the demanding one, who got treated the best. Traci was so nice that she didn't require constant attention. Taryn demanded attention from the moment she was born. And she got it.

None of this is to suggest that one child is better than the other or that we love one more than the other. We love them both for the individual humans that they are. But it does point out that the different temperaments of each child caused us to treat them differently. If you are shy and quiet, your parents will have learned to treat you differently than if you are outgoing. Shy and quiet isn't bad. Outgoing and adventurous isn't better. But each personality will elicit different responses from the people around you, including your parents.

Your personal childhood history also affects the way your parents have learned to respond to you. If you were very sick as a child, you will be treated differently than if you had been healthy. If you exhibited some special gift or talent, your relationship with your parents will be different than if you had not had that gift. Your responsibility as the catalyst for change in your family is to recognize the strengths and weaknesses of your personality and to be aware of how your family responds to them. Your actions and attitudes belong to you, and you have the power to change and control them – but only if you are aware of them.

SPECIAL PARENT NEEDS

Sometimes parents try to live out their own lives in the lives of their children. I met a father who desperately wanted to play football when he was a boy but couldn't even make the team. He was elated when his first child turned out to be a boy. He gave him a toy football right there in the delivery room. From his first steps, the boy was encouraged to learn the skills that would make him a football player. The dad made him practice running, catching, and throwing at every opportunity. As he reached grade school he was involved in little league football. By the time he reached high school he was the best football player in the county.

There was only one problem. He hated football. His interest was in music and the arts. His father insisted that these were sissy pursuits, and when the boy quit the football team to do what he enjoyed doing most, his father disowned him. In the counseling that followed, the dad realized that he desperately wanted his son to be the hero he could never be when he was a boy. Once he realized his mistake, he took steps to correct it. He and his son have a good relationship today.

It is important to remember that that father did not set out to make his son unhappy. For many years he didn't realize how unhappy his son was. He really loved his son. Once the boy understood what caused his father's actions, it was easier to forgive him.

Your parents, too, have needs and problems that affect their relationship with you. If your father spends little time with you, it may be that he is under pressure at his job or under unusual financial stress. If your mother is irritable with you, the cause could be a disagreement with your father rather than anger with you. Be sensitive to your parents' problems and special needs, and it will be easier to understand some of their actions.

THE TEENAGE YEARS

And so we come to the present. Just as your parents have certain problems and needs, so you, in part because of your age, have special problems and needs. You're at that strange and interesting age when you are no longer quite a child but not yet quite an adult. In the process of becoming an adult, you experience feelings and attitudes that add to the complexity of living at peace in your home. Once your only concerns were getting your parents to change that nasty-smelling diaper and feed you. If you screamed real loud, they would feed you that disgusting mashed vegetable stuff and the hunger would go away. Sometimes just looking at that stuff made the hunger go away.

But the years have changed you. Now you're concerned with getting the keys to the Datsun, winning the heart of that special person of the opposite sex, getting good grades in school, and being accepted by your friends. And the years to come will change you even more. Experiencing those changes – experiencing becoming an adult – will affect both you and your parents. You're probably already feeling the natural tendency of adolescents to begin to pull away from your parents. This feeling of independence is an important part of becoming an adult, and you shouldn't feel guilty about it. It's only natural that you want to change your own diaper now and make some decisions on your own. You want to be treated as an equal, but since there is still time to be free and have some fun you don't want to accept all the responsibilities of an adult. Most of all, you want to know that you make a difference and that you are appreciated and loved for who you are.

There is a popular notion that total rebellion is a natural part of growing up. Not true. Your need for independence and freedom does not have to cause a total break between you and your parents. There is a big difference between having a defiant, rebellious attitude against all authority and having a desire to have more personal freedom and control of your life. Only through cooperation and negotiation with your parents will you gain the freedom you so desperately need. You do not have to end up hating your parents to gain the adulthood you are destined to achieve anyway. In most cases the people in the best position to help you through this confusing and difficult time are your parents.

Another dimension of adolescence that adds real interest and challenge to family dynamics is your sudden interest in the opposite sex. Parents who did not show a lot of interest in your friends when you were a child now want to take an active role in deciding who you spend your time with and how much time you spend with them. I think I'm a good parent, but I have this terrible urge to sit at the door with a cannon and a belt full of grenades and interrogate anyone who comes to see my girls. In the chapter on "Dates, Friends, and Twelve-Gauge Shotguns" I will give you some hints on how to get dads like me to unload the cannon and put the grenades away. In the meantime, you'll do well to learn as much as you can about your prehistoric history and about your early life in this world.

Here's that list of questions to ask your parents and relatives:

What kind of person were you in high school?

When you were my age, what did you want to be when you grew up?

What kind of parents were Grandma and Grandpa? Were they strict?

How did you meet Mom/Dad? What was it like dating him/her?

What church did you go to as a teenager? What was it like?

What is our heritage? Where did we come from?

What were my brothers and sisters like when they were babies?

What was I like when I was little?

Were there any really hard times when you were growing up?

Try to find out as much as you can about what makes your parents tick. Remember to listen not only to what your parents say, but also to what they don't say. As they answer your questions, put yourself in their shoes. (Unless they didn't have any and had to walk fifty miles to school through the snow.) If these questions are asked at a relaxed time, with a caring attitude, this exercise could be the first step in seeing your parents in a different light.

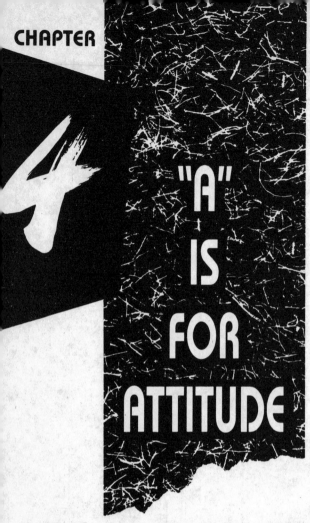

CHAPTER

4

"A"
IS
FOR
ATTITUDE

Vince Lombardi said it, Kermit the frog said it, Solomon said it, and I'll say it: Your attitude affects your behavior. Lombardi knew that all of the training in the world would be of little value unless his team had the right attitude. My attitude affects me so much that it's the first thing I must consider when I get up in the morning. If I start with a bad attitude it affects my whole day. Kermit the frog actually, despite all the rumors to the contrary, thinks Miss Piggy is quite beautiful (I asked him). But he avoids her. Why? Because she has such a terrible attitude. It's your attitude that determines your actions. Over 2500 years before you were even born, King Solomon said, "As man thinks in his heart so he is" (Proverbs 23:7). Men have known about the importance of attitudes since the beginning of time. This chapter will help you decide what is the right attitude for you and give you some helpful suggestions on how you can develop a good attitude.

HOW IMPORTANT IS YOUR ATTITUDE?

All through the Scriptures, from Solomon to Paul to Jesus, the connection between our beliefs, attitudes, and actions is constantly emphasized. Your attitude is determined by what you believe. If you believe that everyone is against you and there is no hope, those beliefs will produce a cynical, negative attitude that will cause you to act as if there were no hope.

Let me illustrate. Imagine you are walking down a path at night. You are alone and believe that the forest is full of terrible creatures planning to make you their late-night snack. As you turn a corner in the path, a harmless old dog crosses in front of you – but it's so dark you can't tell what it is. All you see is a large form moving toward you. At this moment your whole body will get involved. Your eyeballs will send a message to your brain: "It's a bear!" Your feet will not argue with your eyeballs. Your feet will say, "Let's take the body to a new place." Your body will say, "That's a good idea." Then you will burn a hole in the ground getting out of there. It doesn't matter if you are looking at a big dog, a shadow, or a stump. If you think you see a bear, your body will respond exactly as it would if there was a monstrous grizzly standing right in front of you.

I once watched a waitress knock over half the tables in a restaurant when I pulled a puppet rat from under my salad and made it look like it was real. She did not run through the restaurant yelling, "Help! Fake rat! Fake rat!" She believed it was a real rat and her body responded accordingly.

57

No wonder Jesus says so many times, "If you believe me and love me you will obey me." If you really believe that He gave His life for you, it will affect your attitude. How can you help but love Him: "We love Him because he first loved us" (1 John 4:19). If we do love Him we will want to obey Him. If you want to evaluate your *attitude* toward your family and God, ask yourself one question: What does my *behavior* say? Does my behavior reflect a desire to show the love of Christ toward the others in my home, or does it reveal that my major concern is to make life as easy as possible for me? Your attitude toward your family isn't evidenced by the changes you would like to see in *them* – it is reflected by the changes you are willing to make in yourself.

Tammy, a fifteen-year-old girl from the East Coast, spent all of her childhood years in beauty contests – not because she wanted to, but because her mom entered her in every contest within five hundred miles. What little spare time she had was spent in modeling classes and finishing schools. And Tammy *was* exceptionally beautiful and very bright – but more than anything else, she wanted to be a missionary doctor. How did Tammy choose to respond to that difference between her desires and her mother's desires for her? In a way that became a beautiful example of the love of Christ operating in her life. Although she knew that attending beauty contests would not take her any closer to her goal, Tammy continued to attend until she left high school. When I asked her why, she said, "When I walk out on the stage I couldn't care less if I win or lose. What I care about is my mom. Her face almost glows when I'm out there. Something about my participation in these contests makes her happier and more proud than anything I know. If the only price I have to pay to make my mom happy is a few years of preparing for beauty contests, it is well worth the price. I will eventually be able to make my own decisions. Until then I want to make my mom happy."

Because she was mature enough to see the complete picture, Tammy didn't go to the contests grumbling about all the time she was wasting. She realized that, in some way, her mom was reliving her life through her. Because it made her mom happy and made things around home more agreeable, she was glad to do it. I admit that that kind of response is not common. Few people approach life in such a selfless way. But there weren't a lot of Davids either. The whole country was being buffaloed by Goliath. David was the *only* one who believed God enough to act. I spent eighteen years living with my parents and can't remember once trying to figure out what made my parents happy. I can't remember an evening or an hour that I made any effort to make their lives more enjoyable. But God has helped me change. It was also God who helped Tammy. Her belief in Jesus Christ gave her the motive to act in love. Do you believe He loves you and wants the very best for you? Do you believe He has the power to help you, and that He wants to? What you believe about God, about your parents, and about yourself will shape your attitude and affect the outcome of your efforts to live for Christ at home.

WHAT IS THE RIGHT ATTITUDE?

If you believe that your attitude affects your behavior, the next question is: "What is the right attitude?"

The suggestion I am going to make may seem impossible at first. There are adults who will read this and say it is expecting too much from an adult, let alone a teenager. The same criticisms might have been leveled against God had He personally presented David to the Israeli army as the solution to the problem of Goliath. Imagine God calling a meeting of the top brass to announce that He has the solution to the Goliath problem. After a brief pep talk, God brings out David. As the skinny little kid stands in front of these trained professionals, trying to look deadly, God explains that the solution is to send David out alone to fight Goliath with a slingshot. The room would have erupted either into laughter or shouts of total disbelief.

But David *was* God's answer to the Goliath problem. And forty years of living have taught me at least two things. The first is to *never underestimate the ability of a teenager.* From the time of David up to now, teenagers like you have distinguished themselves in history by proving that when they put their minds to something, they can frequently do it better and with more conviction than most adults. There are more kids like Tammy than many realize.

The second thing life has taught me is that *God is not to be laughed at.* He does not suggest ridiculous solutions. He gives us commands that, when obeyed in faith, produce results. The commands may seem ridiculous or even impossible, but the results of obedience will be no less miraculous than David's victory over Goliath.

So what kind of attitude does He want you to have? What kind of attitude will produce the kind of change in you that will make a difference in your family?

Jesus gave the answer to that question in a meeting He had with His disciples shortly before He was crucified. He had just tried to explain to the disciples that He was about to die. The room was full of eleven very depressed and confused men. (Judas had already left the room.) They wondered how He could be speaking of His death when He had so vividly pictured for them the kingdom He was going to set up. Responding to the confusion of His friends, Jesus clearly explained what He wanted them to do. This was His last request to the men He had grown to love so much. Listen to what He said in John 13:33-35: "My children, I will be with you only a little longer ... Where I am going, you cannot come. A new commandment I give you: Love one another. As I have loved you, so you must love one another. All men will know that you are my disciples if you love one another." In this last command given to the men He had trained so carefully lies the secret to the kind of attitude that can make all the difference in the world.

You may say, "Come on, Ken, it can't be that simple." You're right. It's not simple. In fact, it's *impossible* – without His help. It would have been simple if Jesus had said, "My command is that you love each other," and left it at that. You could have made your own definition of love and been home free. But He didn't leave it at that. He said to love each other "as I have loved you." He specifically defined the kind of loving attitude He wanted the disciples to have for one another. Within hours, that kind of love would cause Him to suffer death by crucifixion so that we might be free from our sins. That kind of love has changed the world. It is the only kind of love that can significantly change you and your family. Jesus does not want you to love your parents and your brothers and sisters in just any old way. He wants you to love them in the same way He loved you. And the two most distinguishing elements of His love were: His love was *unconditional* and His love was *fully expressed in action.*

While counseling a teenage girl in Minnesota, I challenged her to go home and love her mom. She and her mother could hardly say more than three words to each other without fighting. The mother showed little maturity; she could have used some counseling herself. I suggested that the girl go home and do all the things she could to express love to her mother. She was back the very next day, her face red with anger and stained with tears. "It didn't work," she sputtered. "I went home last night and immediately cleaned my room and did my homework. I set the table, and after dinner I asked my mom if there was anything else I could do to help. She yelled at me and asked me what I was up to. She accused me of trying to hide something with all my good behavior and demanded to know what it was I had done!"

"So what did you do?" I asked.

She drew herself to her full height and, through her tears, proudly announced, "I threw a dish across the room and said, 'If that's the way you're going to be I just won't do any good things anymore.'" At that she stormed to her room and slammed the door.

Her story pointed out several truths. First, evidently she was not in the habit of doing many loving things at home. Her new behavior shocked her mom into thinking she was up to something. Secondly, her mom was not used to responding to her daughter in a very healthy or mature way. This was brought on by years of bad communication between the two. Third, and most important, my young friend had misunderstood the kind of love that would make a difference. She had gone home thinking that if she loved her mom, her mom would suddenly respond and love her back. Then, if her mom loved her back, she would continue to love her mom. But if her mom did *not* respond in love, she would throw a plate at her and continue to hate her. In Romans 5, the Bible says that God loved us so much that, while we were still sinners, He sent His Son to die for us. Jesus willingly died on the cross for us when we had done nothing to deserve His love. He wants you to demonstrate that same unconditional love to those around you. That's not an easy command to follow. You will fail time and time again. As an adult, I can honestly say that following this command is the most difficult aspect of my Christian life – but that doesn't take away my responsibility to give it my best effort. With God's help, it is possible to grow in this kind of love.

Loving your parents and the other members of your family with this kind of love will not guarantee that they will love you back. But if you persist, it will guarantee that *you* will become more lovable and loving. You will gain the capacity to love even more, expecting even less in return. It will change your family because it will dramatically change you. Is it easy? No. Is it even possible? Yes, but only with God's help. According to Christ's own words, the people around you will take notice of this kind of love. They will say, "That person must be a follower of Christ." "All men will know that you are my disciples if you love one another," Jesus said in John 13:35.

Those who say that teenagers are not mature enough to make such a commitment are wrong. There are thousands of young men and women, like David and Tammy, who are willing to take God at His Word. If you are willing to do the same, you will discover that He is a powerful and faithful God. In the story of David, the greatest miracle wasn't that the giant fell to David's sling. The greatest miracle was that, through the power of God, a teenage boy was willing to do what an army of men were afraid to try. The greatest miracle He will do for you will not be to make your problems go away, but to give you the faith and courage to become the key to solving them.

CHAPTER

5

GETTING YOUR ACT TOGETHER

I hope I've shown you that your attitude is important. I've also talked about the kind of attitude that will make a difference. So now you're probably asking: "How can I change my attitude?"

Bad attitudes are a vicious cycle. They cause bad actions, which result in conflict, which causes more bad attitudes, which lead to more bad actions, and so on. To change your attitude, you have to get off the vicious cycle – and onto the victory cycle.

A vicious cycle is characterized by complaining, yelling, criticizing, lying, and attempting to escape. These actions feed on each

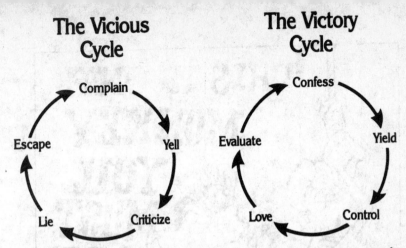

The Vicious Cycle

Complain → Yell → Criticize → Lie → Escape → Complain

The Victory Cycle

Confess → Yield → Control → Love → Evaluate → Confess

other and make it hard to break the pattern. In a vicious cycle, you find yourself constantly complaining about your personal situation: "If I only had a father like Traci's dad, then things would be different."

I had just finished speaking on family relationships to an audience of over two thousand people. While signing autographs, a girl about fifteen years old came up and grabbed my hand. "Oh, Mr. Davis," she said, "I wish I had a father as wonderful as you." I was about to reply when I heard a strange noise and looked down to see my daughter, Traci, sticking her finger in her throat and making little gagging sounds. She knew better than anyone in the room that I was not a perfect father. There are no perfect fathers. There are no perfect mothers or brothers and sisters – only human beings who will make many mistakes along the way. Complaining always provokes statements like:

> *"If only they cared."*
> *"No one understands me."*
> *"Why am I always the one to blame?"*

Complaining leads to yelling:

> *"I hate you."*
> *"You don't love me."*
> *"Okay, if that's the way you want it."*

65   Getting Your Act Together

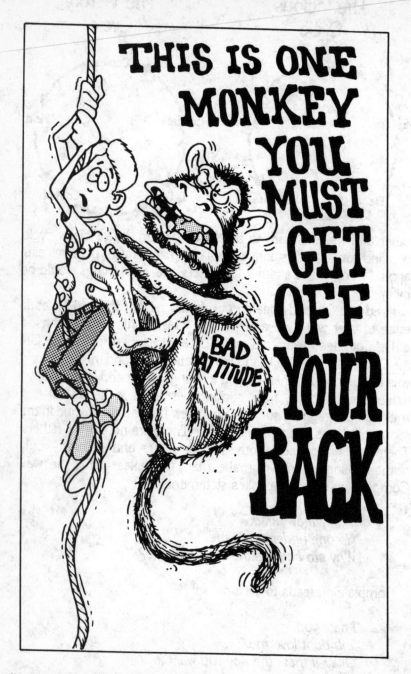

THIS IS ONE MONKEY YOU MUST GET OFF YOUR BACK

BAD ATTITUDE

Even though you don't mean it, you yell it anyway. Criticizing others is an intricate part of the vicious cycle. Mom is too picky. Dad is too strict. Brother is too dumb. Sister is too much of a pain. If you begin to believe all this, it will be impossible to see any of the solutions that will lead to constructive change.

Lying is the next part of the cycle. You lie to yourself and everyone else by implying, *I'm okay, everybody else is rotten.* Then, rather than face the problem head on, you move to the next part of the cycle: *escape!* Some teenagers try to escape by drowning themselves in drugs, parties, television, or music. Some just go into hibernation in their rooms. Others do anything – as long as it keeps them out of the house. No matter what means of escape you choose, the problems that started the vicious cycle in the first place will not go away. They get worse. That just gives you more reason to complain, yell, criticize, lie, and escape, and the cycle goes on and on and on.

The answer is to switch cycles. Stop this un-merry-go-round and change from a vicious cycle to a victory cycle. The steps that make up a victory cycle are these: Confess, yield, control, love, and evaluate. This cycle also perpetuates itself, but rather than leading to destruction, bitterness, and conflict, it changes your attitude and leads to positive actions. Look at each step in the victory cycle carefully. And remember this: Once you get on this cycle, God will keep it spinning. It's up to you to *want* to be on it enough to hang on.

CONFESS

Hundreds of times I've heard people say, "But I can't help the way I feel!" That's true. You can't help the way you feel – right now.

But you *can* make up your mind that you don't want to feel that way. In fact, that's one of the first steps in changing the way you feel: You have to *want* to change. It's easier to keep on hating and rebelling and disliking the people in your family than it is to decide that you're willing to change. After all, in order to change you have to admit that you are wrong. That's hard, especially if you feel that other members of the family are wrong or that you're being treated unfairly. And that's precisely why you must stop concentrating on the faults of others: As long as you do, you won't be willing to deal with your own.

If your attitudes are wrong, you must admit that they're wrong and confess them as sin. That's not easy. The simple act of saying to God, "I'm sorry, God, for my sin" is extremely difficult. Maybe that's because Satan recognizes this as the first important step in the healing of your family. Maybe it's because we don't trust God and are afraid of what He will do. I always get tickled when someone says they're afraid of what God will do if He finds out they've sinned. I get a mental picture of God with a shocked look on His face, slapping His forehead and saying, "Oh, no – you've got to be kidding!" God is not suprised when we tell Him what we have done or how we feel. He already knows. He keeps on loving us the whole time. His heart is filled with great joy when we trust Him enough to come to Him and say, "Father, I have sinned. Please forgive me."

If I saw one of my daughters do something wrong I would not be pleased. But if they tried to *hide* it from me, I would be very distressed. The day they came to confess what they had done would be a happy day for me. Sometimes your parents will blow up when you confess something you have done. That's because you have surprised them, and they are disappointed and angry. The difference with God is that you can never surprise Him. He knows. He is only waiting for you to trust Him enough to confess so that He can assure you that you are forgiven and can begin to use His power to correct the problem. The Bible says, "If we confess our sins, He is faithful and just and will forgive us our sins and purify us from all unrighteousness" (1 John 1:9). Are you willing to confess any of your attitudes or actions that are preventing the kind of healing God would love to do in your life and family? Take a moment to identify those negative attitudes and actions as sin and confess them to God.

YIELD

The second action in a victory cycle is to yield.

Once you recognize areas of your life that need work, there is a real tendency to puff your chest out and proclaim, "I'm never going to do *that* again." But stop and think a minute: How many times have you said that about some aspect of your life, and then kept on doing it? Even the apostle Paul experienced this. It is our nature to want to reach down and pull ourselves up by our bootstraps. Unfortunately, the only thing you get by pulling on your bootstraps is broken bootstraps. The "I can do it myself" attitude will eventually lead to discouragement and failure, but it's hard to give that attitude up because we think if we *don't* handle it ourselves, it won't get handled. We don't really trust God to handle things, in other words. And that makes it hard to yield, because yielding is the process of (1) admitting that you are unable in your own strength to solve your problems and then (2) giving them completely to Him to handle. God, then, is free to give you the strength to accomplish what you could not do on your own. Yielding is an act of faith. It's saying to God, "I can't do it Lord, but You can – so it's yours." If confession is admitting to God that we are weak, then yielding is trusting Him to be strong where we are weak.

There was a man standing near the edge of a cliff. As he stood admiring the view, the ground beneath his feet gave way. He fell several hundred feet and, by some miracle, managed to grab a small branch growing from the side of the cliff. His feet dangled

69

over a thousand feet of empty space, and there was no way to climb back up. He was quickly losing his grip. In panic he screamed, "Help! Help! Is anybody up there?"

God heard the man's cry and shouted down in His most majestic voice, "I am God, and I will help you."

"Throw down a rope!" the man yelled as his grip weakened.

"I don't have a rope," replied God.

In desperation the man yelled, "Can you help me?"

"Yes," God replied, "I can help you if you will trust me."

"Oh, I trust you. I trust you," the man said, "but please hurry."

God said, "If you trust me, let go of the branch."

There was only a short pause before the man screamed, "Is there anybody else up there?"

Yielding is like letting go of the branch. It is the act of putting it all in God's hands. Just as it is only through His power that our sins are forgiven, it is only through His power that we can conquer that sin. Throughout the book of Romans, Paul explains how we are to deal with sin. In Romans 12:1,2, he encourages us to yield our bodies to God. He gets even more specific in Romans 6:12-14 where he says we must offer the parts of our body to God. If you can sincerely pray asking God to take the areas of your life that are weak and through His power make them strong, He will give *you* the power to make the changes that need to be made. There are no short cuts.

The second step in the victory cycle is to yield. Leave it out, and you won't be on the victory cycle at all.

CONTROL

The third step on the victory cycle is to control the influences that affect us. That's not easy. It requires a conscious decision to saturate yourself in the Word of God and to refuse to allow the negative influences that are everywhere to bombard your mind.

For example: A lot of what you see on TV and in the movies

encourages rebellion toward your parents. Much of it suggests that your parents are the enemy, or that they're just plain stupid. You are encouraged to deceive and manipulate them to get what you want. Being continually exposed to such influences – whether you *think* you're paying any attention to those voices or not – will affect your ability to think clearly. What we choose to read, watch, and listen to has a profound impact on our attitudes and will eventually affect our behavior.

The first place to go to discover the positive attitudes and actions that will keep us on the right track is – you guessed it – the Bible. I can't emphasize enough the importance of reading from God's Word every day.

Psalm 1 shows us that God richly blesses those who delight in seeking direction from His Word. The writer warns us to control the effects of ungodly influences on our lives. For instance: How many times have you had friends tell you to kiss your parents off? These kids refer to their parents – with a curse – as the old lady or the old man. They hate their parents and encourage you to do the same. At times, even adults may encourage you to write off your mom and dad. On the victory cycle, you control your input by avoiding such counsel. ("Blessed is the man who does not walk in the counsel of the wicked or stand in the way of sinners" – Psalm 1:1.)

God also promises to bless you if you refuse to scorn and criticize. ("Blessed is the man who does not ... sit in the seat of mockers" – Psalm 1:1.)

But the real key to success is found in verses 2-6 of Psalm 1: "But his delight is in the law of the Lord, and on his law he meditates day and night. He is like a tree planted by streams of water, which yields its fruit in season and whose leaf does not wither. Whatever he does prospers." Not only will you find it easier to keep your attitude and thoughts in control by allowing God's Word to saturate your mind, but according to this Scripture, you will be rewarded with a prosperous and fruitful life.

Take time each day to read the Bible, asking God's Spirit to show you how to live that day. Claim all His promises and pray for the wisdom to apply what you read to your life at home. Then, as the day progresses, keep those things on your mind. That is what is meant by meditating on God's Word. Romans 12:2 puts it this way: "Do not conform any longer to the pattern of this world, but be transformed by the renewing of your mind. Then you will be able to test and approve what God's will is – his good, pleasing and perfect will." Let me paraphrase that verse: *Give God control of your attitudes and actions by refusing to allow the world to press you into its way of thinking. Instead, transform your mind by allowing it to be influenced by a constant exposure to God's Word. That will allow the desires of your God to always be close to your heart. You will know what He wants.* When you practice control rather than accepting whatever comes your way, you select the input that influences your life. You seek God's will by exposing yourself daily to His Word and applying that Word where you live.

Another important step in maintaining control is to develop a circle of friends who know that you want to live for Christ. They will be your home base.

Your home base? Sure. As a child, I loved the game of tag. In tag there was always a home base. When I was so tired from running that I could hardly stand up, I would run to home base. While touching home base I could rest and not worry about being tagged. You couldn't stay there forever, but at least you could gather your strength for the next round. A group of your peers and some trustworthy adults who know that you are trying to make some changes in your life can be like a home base. They can provide a place where you can cry when things are tough, where you can share new triumphs, and where you can seek advice and counsel.

Don't underestimate the value of your pastor or youth pastor in this role. They would be delighted to help you. They can encourage you when you need it and help you see areas that need improvement. In addition to the help that your regular church meetings can provide, they may even be able to help you establish a support group of your peers who are facing the same challenge.

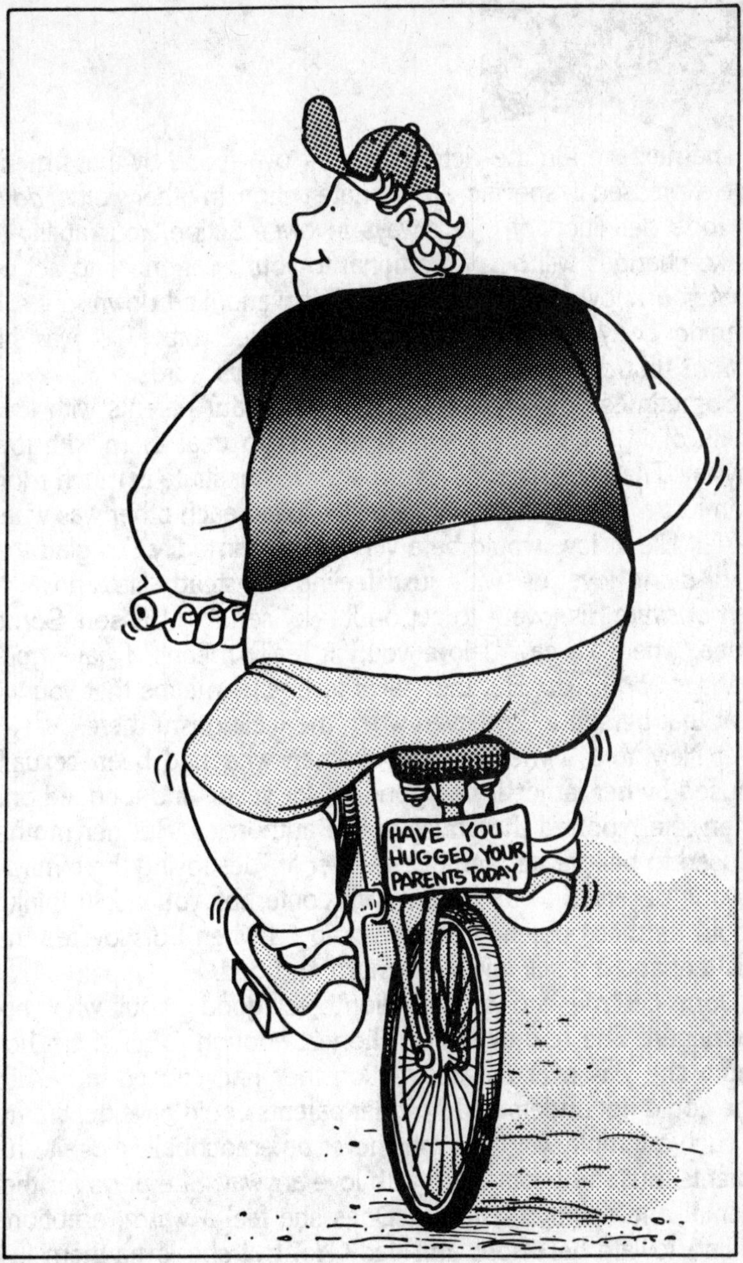
HAVE YOU
HUGGED YOUR
PARENTS TODAY

LOVE

The next step in the victory cycle is love – and by that I mean love expressed in specific, appropriate action. In other words, *do it.*

God's definition of love always involves action. Your ability to make changes will be proportional to your willingness to act on what you know is right. David would have looked downright silly running away from the giant yelling, "I feel brave." It was his *actions* that demonstrated his bravery, not his words.

Sometimes you won't feel like treating your parents with love. That's okay. What God wants is for you to treat them with love anyway. The love that God asks us to demonstrate is much more than just a feeling. If the only time we loved each other was when we felt like it, love would be a very rare commodity. I'm glad that God didn't love us with just feelings. Instead, He chose to *demonstrate* His love – to act on it – by sending His son. Sometimes, when we say, "I love you," it really means, *I have good feelings about you.* But the real "I love you" means that you will treat that person in love even when the feeling isn't there.

In New York, I met a young woman who had been sexually abused by her father. It had gone on for years, and it ended only when she reported the abuse to the authorities. But her mother refused to believe her and blamed her for destroying the family. If anyone deserved to be treated with contempt, you would think it would be these parents. So I was moved when I discovered that this teenage girl *still loved* her mom and dad.

Don't get me wrong. She didn't feel good about what had happened. She had even been honest enough to tell them how angry she was over the destruction they had caused in her life. She could not understand how her parents could have treated her in such a terrible way. She may never be emotionally close to her parents, but she treats them with love anyway. She prays for their mental and spiritual recovery. Does she feel a warm, emotional feeling toward her mom and dad? No. But she loves them in a more real way than some children who have a warm fuzzy feeling toward their parents but never express that love in action.

When you are faced with the challenge of loving someone who is not lovable, you have two options. You can treat them with love and get *better,* or you can choose the vicious cycle and get *bitter.* Love that is not expressed in action is not love. Jesus did not feel good about going to the cross. He even asked His Father whether there was any other way. We had done nothing to deserve His sacrifice, yet His love caused Him to die for us. In doing so He not only provided an example we could follow, but He used the power of love to defeat sin. As a forgiven child of His, He makes that same power available to you. Do something today to express love to your parents.

EVALUATE

The last step in the victory cycle is *evaluation.* This allows you to give thanks to God for the growth in your life, see the changes that are taking place, and discover new areas of challenge to work on.

Brian decided to get his act together and become the center of Christ's love in his home. So he looked at his life and saw that, of all the areas that could use improvement, his temper probably topped the list. He admitted to himself that his wild flare-ups of temper were sinful, confessed it to God, and yielded that area of his life totally to the Lord. Over the next few weeks he eliminated from his life the influences that encouraged his angry outbursts, and he also sought counsel from his youth pastor. He shared his desire to conquer this problem with two of his closest Christian friends, and they agreed to help him. Then Brian began actively using God's power to respond to his parents differently than in the past. He failed on several occasions, but he didn't give up. Instead, he asked for forgiveness and continued to give each situation to Christ.

Getting Your Act Together

Then one day Brian's father accused him of something he had not done. It was a struggle not to lash out in anger and hatred as he had done so many times before. But even in the midst of his father's untrue accusations, Brian was able to control his temper and keep quiet. By the time his father had finished raving, Brian was very angry – but he quietly claimed his innocence. His father was so surprised by his son's calm reply that he asked for an explanation, which gave Brian the chance to logically explain the mistake. His father accepted the explanation and apologized.

But that apology was not what Brian called his friends together to praise the Lord about. What Brian was excited about was that he had been able to treat his father with love, even while feeling angry about being falsely accused. As the boys thanked God for His faithfulness, Brian realized that the problem with his father had come up in the first place because of Brian's own laziness and undependability. He had neglected to do a job that his dad had asked him to do weeks before. Here was another area that could be submitted to the victory cycle. There, with his friends, Brian confessed his lazy attitude as sin, and the process started again. As Brian left that day, his heart was glad that the challenge to live for Christ every day of his life, and especially the challenge to live for Him at home, would last a lifetime. He looked forward to the next Goliath.

Unless you take time, like Brian, to evaluate your progress, you'll quickly become discouraged. After I spoke at camp one summer, a girl came to me in tears. She felt like nothing had changed in her life since becoming a Christian three years before.

"Tell me what your life was like *before* you became a Christian," I said.

As she reviewed the past three years, her face began to shine. She realized there *had* been some major changes in her life. Three years before, she had constantly been running away from home. But she hadn't run away once since trusting Christ. Three years before, she would never have considered attending a Christian camp – yet here she was seeking opportunities to know more about the Lord. Most significantly, three years before, she wouldn't have had the slightest concern about the quality of her spiritual growth, yet now she sat before me with an open Bible wanting more than anything to know that Christ was making a difference in her life.

Evaluation is the process of stopping along the journey long enough to look back and see how far you have come. When you look only at how far you have to go, it can seem hopeless. But when you pause to look back, you realize you can go at least that far again, and then at least that far again. Then you can find the strength to forget what is behind and look forward to the challenges of tomorrow.

Remember David? When you read about David's earlier life, you realize that he had many memories of God's faithfulness to encourage him as he ran toward that giant. He wasn't willing to just sit around with the guys, bragging about the lion and the bear. There was a giant that needed fixin', and David knew that God had the tools to do the job.

Evaluation also allows you to see where you must go from here. Paul says, "Forgetting what is behind and straining toward what is ahead, I press on toward the goal to win the prize for which God has called me heavenward in Christ Jesus" (Philippians 3:13-14). Just as Brian was able to see a new area of his life he could bring under the Lordship of Christ, evaluation will allow you to see new areas of your life you can confess and yield to Him.

The secret, then, to developing a Christlike attitude is to first get off the vicious cycle by refusing to complain, yell, criticize, lie, or escape. Then get on the victory cycle by confessing those negative attitudes, yeilding them to the control of Christ, controlling your influences, actively treating your parents with love, and evaluating your progress. The same God who gave you the desire to follow Him in obedience will not leave you on your own: "Being confident of this, that he who began a good work in you will carry it on to completion until the day of Christ Jesus" (Philippians 1:6). We struggle. We occasionally fail. But God is not going to give up on us.

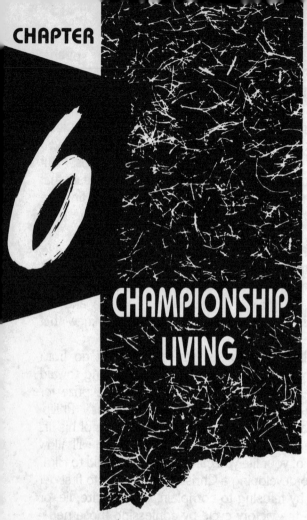

CHAPTER

6

CHAMPIONSHIP LIVING

Once you're on the victory cycle, you can take the offense and move ahead with confidence. How? By doing what God asks – that you yield only to Him. Never to the enemy and never to the pressures around you. When you've yielded to Him, He gives you the power to accomplish what you could never do without Him.

And God wants you to use that power offensively, not defensively. Webster's definition of defense is: "to guard against attack, to defend by fortification." God doesn't want you to use His power only to build a wall so that you are protected from harm. He also wants you to use it to make an impact on your world. He doesn't want you huddled in fear inside some spiritual fortification. He wants you to be outside the walls, moving forward.

Many people live their lives defensively – just enough work in school to keep from failing, just enough effort at the job to keep from being fired, just enough help at home to keep from being grounded, and just enough faith to keep from going to hell. What a sad way to live.

David surely didn't live that way. He didn't gather the army together to build a big fort so Goliath couldn't get at them. He didn't dig a huge pit, put sharp sticks at the bottom, and then sit back and hope the giant would fall in. He didn't lay land mines, or dig a fox hole to defend his ground. He attacked! The Bible says he ran *toward* Goliath.

The apostle Paul didn't say, "I sit on my backside and try hard to keep Satan from getting to me." He said, "I press on toward the goal to win the prize for which God has called me" (Philippians 3:14). Paul was always on the front lines, not only presenting the claims of Christ, but also striving for excellence in his own life.

As I studied the Bible, I was amazed to discover that Jesus spent no time defending Himself, not even when He was hanging on the cross. Rather than trying to defend Himself from those who were killing Him, He asked His Father to forgive them. Rather than concentrating on the incredible physical and emotional pain that racked His body, He met the spiritual needs of a thief who hung next to Him. From the time of His birth, Christ was attacked from every side – yet He always moved forward to accomplish His mission.

This chapter will help you establish an offensive strategy in your home. Unless you've taken the steps outlined in the previous chapters, you dare not move ahead. Only when you're confident that God is providing the power can you take an offensive position. Without recognizing Him as your living Savior and trusting totally in Him for your strength, you are attempting the impossible. Your home life does not have to be a series of defensive reactions. It can be a winning adventure. On your own, you're no match for what lies ahead. With Him, you can move forward with confidence.

The most exciting moments of a football game are when your team has the ball and is advancing down the field. The steps required for you to make exciting progress in living for Christ at home are not much different from those taken by a winning football team. They must think *touchdown*, they must have a *game plan*, and they must *play by the rules.*

THINK TOUCHDOWN

In other words, think positive. And I don't mean the kind of positive thinking that says, "If you think about good things, then only good things will happen to you." You won't find that in the Bible, and you won't see it in real life either. You've probably known good people who were positive thinkers and yet had tragedy strike their personal lives. Paul said, "In all things God works for the good of those who love him [and] have been called according to His purpose" (Romans 8:28). He did not say, "Only good things will happen to those who love him." *All* the things that happen to you – difficult or easy, happy or sad – He will use to bring you closer to His good and perfect will. As you try to live for Christ, you'll find hassles, setbacks, failures, and temptation all along the way. That doesn't mean you're failing. It may even mean you're making progress; after all, only those that move forward meet resistance. Be encouraged: *God will use everything that comes your way to move you closer to Him.*

The kind of positive thinking I'm talking about is the kind that Solomon spoke of when he said, "As a man thinks in his heart so he is" (Proverbs 23:7). If you constantly think of yourself as a poor suffering child who is trapped under the rule of unfair parents, with brothers and sisters who have been put on this earth only to make your life miserable, then you're practicing what I call *defensive thinking*. Keep it up and you'll always act like a poor suffering child, just trying to hold down the fort until Jesus comes. On the

other hand, if you believe that each day will bring both happy and difficult circumstances that can be used to demonstrate the power of God, you'll live like it.

When a football team takes the field, they must always think offensively. Imagine a coach giving his team this pep talk: "Okay, boys," he whines, "we haven't got a chance today. The other team is against us. The officials are nearsighted and favor our opponents. So what can we do? Let's just go out there and try to keep the other team from scoring. Try not to get hurt, but if you *do* feel any pain, just quit."

That coach wouldn't last fifteen minutes, and his team would never win a game. On a successful team, the central idea in the mind of every player is to *win*. And you only win by making touchdowns. On a winning team, even the defensive squad tries to get the ball back so the offense can score points. To win, you have to have a positive attitude; you have to want to move the ball forward.

In the 1987 Western Division play-offs, the Denver Broncos were playing the Cleveland Browns for the championship. It was a very physical game, and with five minutes left in the fourth quarter the score was 20 to 13 in favor of Cleveland. As a result of a muffed kick-off, Denver ended up with the ball on their own 1½-yard line. They had 98½ yards to go in five minutes to tie the game and gain a chance to win in overtime.

As they huddled, facing what seemed like an impossible position, Keith Bishop turned to his teammates and said, "Okay, boys, now we got 'em right where we want them. If everybody does their job, good things will happen." Now that's a positive attitude. I am sure that attitude was part of the reason that they drove all the way down the field, scored a touchdown, and won the game in overtime.

Does this positive thinking help you with the challenge that you face at home? It can – if you can learn to apply it to three areas of your life.

First, *you must have a positive concept of yourself.* Don't think of yourself as a helpless child in a hopeless situation. See yourself as a giantkiller, empowered by a powerful God. You were created with special attention by a mighty Lord. He designed you to accomplish what no one else on the face of the earth can accomplish. He loved you enough to send His only son to die in your place. Finally, He offers you every ounce of power you will need to live for Him. No, you are *not* a helpless child! You are the child of a King. Because of Him, you can accomplish the impossible. So, because of Him, you must recognize your value and ability.

Second, *you must develop a positive attitude toward your family.* Don't concentrate on their negative behavior. If you look for the negative, you'll find it. Decide instead to look for the good in your family, and you'll find things you never knew existed. Listen to the advice Paul gave to some Christian friends who were having a hard time getting along: "Rejoice in the Lord always. I will say it again: Rejoice! Let your gentleness be evident to all. The Lord is near. Do not be anxious about anything, but in everything, by prayer and petition, with thanksgiving, present your requests to God. And the peace of God, which transcends all understanding, will guard your hearts and your minds in Christ Jesus. Finally, brothers, whatever is true, whatever is noble, whatever is right, whatever is pure, whatever is lovely, whatever is admirable – if anything is excellent or praiseworthy – think about such things" (Philippians 4:4--8). That kind of thinking can turn your attitude inside out.

Third, *you must think positively about the future.* Don't be satisfied with the status quo, but decide to show your family the love of Christ in every way you possibly can. Be aggressive. Instead of looking at your giant as an impossible threat from which you must hide, look at it as an opportunity – for slingshot practice.

HAVE A GAME PLAN

If you want to move forward, you need a game plan. You must set measurable goals.

According to the story, there was a freshman football coach who gave his team the football and said, "All right, guys – go out there and make a touchdown!" By halftime they were behind 114 to 0. The coach spent most of his locker-room pep talk chewing them out. As he stood there, yelling for touchdowns, he saw a hand go up in the back. It was his quarterback.

"Coach, may I ask a question?" asked the young man.

"What is it?" the coach responded gruffly.

With a sheepish look, the quarterback asked, "What's a touchdown?"

The team had stumbled around the field for two quarters not knowing what they were trying to accomplish. *You must know exactly what you're trying to do if you expect to make any progress.* If you aim at nothing you will probably hit nothing, and if you happen to accomplish something along the way you probably won't know what you did or how you did it. When the coach explained that a touchdown consisted of carrying the ball across the opposing team's goal, his team was ecstatic. Now they had a game plan. Before, they had simply been trying to keep the ball away from all those bad men who chased them whenever they picked it up.

This chapter and the ones before it have been talking about *preparing yourself* for making a difference in your family. The rest of the book will discuss how to *use* what you've learned to this point. As you'll discover, it's not as easy as just saying, "I'm going to learn to love my parents more." You must define what that means. How will you *know* that you're loving them more? What measurable things can you do to show that love? What is your *goal?*

The answers to those questions will be different for each person who reads this book. David's goal was to kill the giant. In the previous chapter, Brian's goal was to control his temper. Your goal may be to overcome a bad attitude or to understand your parents. Regardless of what goal you choose to start with, it's important to remember that a single touchdown doesn't win a game. In reality, we all have the same game-winning goal: to please God in every aspect of our life. But how do we measure progress toward that goal? By one personal achievement (touchdown) at a time.

Sometimes our progress seems so small we have to measure it in mere yards, or even inches. If, for instance, your usual response to disagreeing with your parents is to tell them you hate them, and you temper that response just once, then you have gained an inch. Give thanks. It's better than losing ground. Overcoming your temper completely may be like a ten-yard gain or even a touchdown.

The game is won by making progress a little at a time. Even so, many teenagers get discouraged and give up because their progress isn't dramatic. Sister Teresa, a compassionate nun who has a ministry with starving people, was once asked, "How can you possibly hope to feed all the hungry people in the world?"

Her response was, "One person at a time."

With all of the changes that need to be made in your home, how can you even make a dent? The answer is one little step at a time. Like a kind word where none existed before. A hug for someone with whom you usually fight. A promise to try harder. A commitment to study God's Word. Those are the little gains from which victory is made.

I learned this the hard way playing tennis with a friend. I was leading five games to love. (Love means zip, for all you nontennis fans.) In other words, I only had to win one more game and I would win the set. Before he started what I thought would be his last serve, my friend laid down his racket and said, "I only have to win seven games in a row in order to win this set."

I thought, *That's impossible.*

Then he walked to the net, looked me right in the eye, and said, "I will win those games one at a time."

I thought, *Fat chance.*

"I'll start by winning this point," he said as he walked back to the base line.

Well, he might get one point, I thought. He then proceeded to pick up his racket and win the set – one point at a time.

Choose a goal! Get something out there to aim at. Then chop

that goal into bite-size hunks and work toward it day by day, hour by hour, minute by minute.

Don't know what goal to shoot for? One of the reasons I've stressed the importance of reading the Word of God daily is that it's the best source for finding goals. While you read it, God's Spirit will speak to your heart, pointing out areas that need work (I know that sounds mystical, but trust me.). A nice side benefit is that the Bible is also the single most powerful source of encouragement, and when we're working on family problems we definitely need encouragement.

Besides that, here are some specific suggestions:

SUGGESTED WEEKLY GOALS

I will not speak harshly to my parents.

I will not fight with my brothers and sisters.

I will treat my brothers and sisters with love, even when they deserve to be hung by the toes until red.

I will make my bed every day.

I will spend thirty minutes each day reading the Bible, learning how God wants me to think and act.

I will clean my room every week.

Every day, I will do one task that needs to be done without being asked.

I will take the time to talk to my parents about how I can be a better son/daughter.

I will do my homework without being asked.

I will tell Mom and Dad that I love them at least once every day.

I will not give up trying to understand my folks when they seem unreasonable.

I'll show love to my brother/sister by spending some time doing something they enjoy. I will not allow anger to rule my tongue.

If I have deceived my parents, I will admit it to them and tell them how I plan to go about cleaning up my act.

I will pray for the other members of my family every day.

Decide what your goal for the next week will be – maybe one of the ones I suggested, maybe one of your own – and write it out on a piece of paper. Resist the temptation to say, *I need help in all these areas, so I'll work on all of them at once.* It's much more encouraging to set a small goal and accomplish it than to tackle too much and end up feeling like a failure. But if you *do* fail at your goal, remember that God is forgiving – He'll be right there to pick you up and take you on.

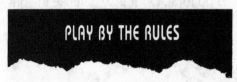

PLAY BY THE RULES

Since I've been using football to illustrate the importance of offensive strategy, here's another example. I was at a college football game just the other day, watching in dismay as the teams piled up more than three hundred yards in penalties. The game was one of the worst I've ever seen. There was no winner. One of the teams simply lost worse than the other.

I have seen many teams lose because of penalties – and I've also watched young men and women ruin their lives because of penalties. The point is that if you desire to make some changes in the way things go at home, you have to learn to play by the rules. It is only within the system that you will find the freedom to make changes. The smart teenager learns as much as possible about how the system in his home works and then uses that knowledge to move ahead. If you refuse to learn the rules, you'll never win the game.

Every family operates differently. Some parents allow children to openly question their decisions; others don't. Some families tolerate a certain amount of fighting among the children; others ground you for it. *Know the rules* – otherwise, you'll surely break them at some point and be confused and angry much of the rest of the time.

Once you know the rules, make a commitment to live by them. Remember, disobedience is not an option for the Christian teenager. The penalty is much worse than just being grounded or having to go to jail without passing go or collecting two hundred dollars. The penalty is that you harden a bit of your heart. You get bitter instead of better, and very quickly you find yourself on the vicious cycle.

It comes down to this: If you are willing to think positively about yourself, your family, and your challenge, if you set measurable goals, and if you make an effort to know the rules and live by them, you'll be in a position to go for it. Don't play defense in your family – play offense.

Part II
Going into Action

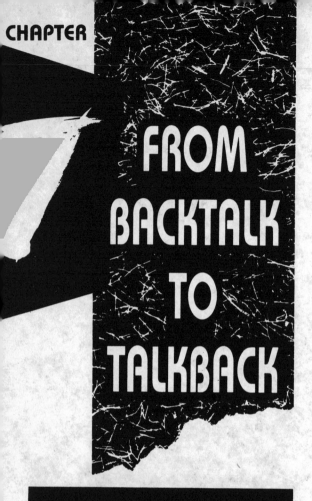

CHAPTER

FROM BACKTALK TO TALKBACK

SILENCE IS NOT GOLDEN

It was 1985. I was flying in cold gray clouds at seven thousand feet, and I knew I was in trouble. An inch of deadly ice protruded from the leading edge of the airplane's wings. Icing like that had killed many pilots in the past, but I thought I could deal with it – so I began to climb.

Suddenly I smelled smoke. Within seconds, the white, acrid smoke from burning wire filled the cockpit and stung my eyes.

Now the situation was critical; there's nothing more dangerous for a pilot than an in-flight fire. When it's combined with airframe icing in instrument conditions, the odds against survival are great.

Wasting no time, I radioed for help and received an immediate response. The controllers on the ground knew that my situation was grave. Because of the fire, I'd had to shut off the electrical instruments I desperately needed to fly in the clouds. I was flying blind in an airplane that was quickly turning into a popsicle. I had only one hope for survival: my link of communication with the controllers. I had to keep them appraised of my situation, and they had to keep me informed as to where I might land. Most of the airports within easy distance were closed because of the weather. Minneapolis had the nearest airport with the radar to guide me down and the fire equipment to assist if I was unsuccessful. By the time I reached Minneapolis, there would be no fuel left for a second try.

Even though it was a life-and-death situation, I felt assured that the controllers and I could work together to find the best solution to this mess. But that assurance was quickly shaken. In order to give me proper radar coverage, the controller asked me to change to a different radio frequency. He told me that I would be talking to people who would guide me all the way down to the runway. He encouraged me to stay calm, wished me luck, and gave me the new frequency. I quickly tuned it in and asked for help. Dead silence.

For five minutes (it seemed like five years), I called for help. Without communication, I was facing certain death. I didn't have enough gas to get to clear weather and I didn't have the instrumentation I needed to land in this weather. Only communication with the controller could save my life. I switched back to the old frequency. No response.

Now I was terrified. I tried other frequencies, hoping I might run into one that would get me through. In my panic, I forgot the frequency I had originally been assigned. As I frantically twisted the dial my earphones were suddenly filled with the sweetest sound in all the earth: someone calling the numbers of my plane.

The controller carefully guided my plane through the fog to a tense but safe landing at Minneapolis International Airport. If communication had not been restored that day, chances are great I would have become a sad statistic of what happens when people don't talk.

I'm sure you see the point. Just as our survival depends on good communication, your ability to live at peace with your parents will depend on establishing good quality communication. It's the vital link with your parents that must not be broken. But good communication doesn't come naturally. It's a skill to be learned. This chapter will help you understand the absolute importance of this link and will teach you how to develop good lines of communication and keep them open.

Even animals must communicate to survive. God enabled them to signal a wide range of emotions, and they usually continue to communicate those emotions – loud and long – even when angry or hurt. Frankly, that makes them seem smarter than humans. After all, when we're upset with one another we often stop communicating. That's like deliberately turning off the radios in a burning airplane.

Both parents and kids are guilty of this. When there's trouble, if your parents don't banish you to your room to sit alone, chances are you will run there on your own and slam the door on any possibility of talking it out. It's true that there are times when it's wise get alone and cool off before you speak, but even then it's best to make it clear that you're willing to talk as soon as you have yourself under control. Keep the lines of communication open. Even if those lines are shredded, guard the last threads with all of your energy.

HOW TO TALK TO YOUR PARENTS

Communication is a two-way street.
Just as in the true story of my emergency, effective communica-

tion requires input from both parties. But, for a variety of reasons, parents are sometimes reluctant to take those first steps to get it started. So it's up to you. I don't suggest you walk up to your dad and say "Come on, Pop, open up and tell me what you are feeling." Neither would you start by telling your parents you think they run your home like a concentration camp. They won't respond by begging you to show them where they went wrong. Instead, they will put another strand of barbed wire around the perimeter. So, if you want to improve communication in your family, how do you start it?

Share Your Life

Start by being more open. How much of your life do you share with your parents?

Several years ago I took three high-school seniors on a canoe trip. The first night out a storm blew our canoes away while we slept. We were stranded on a small island for hours before flagging down a forest ranger who radioed for help. An airplane found our canoes undamaged on the opposite end of the lake.

The next day a boy named Jim caught a nineteen-pound fish. It took almost forty-five minutes to get it landed. We couldn't get it into the canoe, so we paddled to shore while Jim continued to fight it. On shore, we all jumped out and flopped on top of this monster fish. It looked bigger than our canoe. Jim just kept jumping up and down yelling, "Can you believe that?"

One day I came back to our camp with an armload of firewood to discover all three boys swimming twenty yards from shore with their clothes on. Sitting by the campfire, eating our dinner, and watching the boys swim, was the biggest bear I had ever seen in my life. When that bear looked at me and made a little woof sound, I went swimming with the boys.

That week was an incredible adventure. We tipped the canoe over with all our gear on board; we had to take shelter to avoid a

93

lightning storm; we ran rapids that scared us to death; we dove off huge cliffs decorated with Indian paintings; and we caught enough fish to feed an army. When I brought the boys home, Jim's dad met us at a restaurant. "How was your week, Jim?" he asked.

I was amazed when Jim answered, "Aw, it was all right."

All right? It had been fantastic! The next day Jim would be bragging to all his friends about the great things he'd experienced – but he refused to share that happiness with his dad.

The same thing happened to me the other day when I called my daughter, Traci, from the West Coast. "How was school today?" I asked.

"Same as usual," was her reply.

Later I discovered that one of Traci's classmates had been hit by a car that day. She had been standing right there when it happened. If the day was "same as usual," there must be a lot of bodies in the street outside that school.

One of the greatest ways to open the lines of communication with your parents is by beginning to share your life with them. Why not jot down a couple of the day's highlights and share them with your parents when you get home from school? I love it when Traci and Taryn come home and tell me about the special things that happened that day. Okay – I admit that sometimes their timing is bad. If they try to get my attention while I'm watching the news, talking on the telephone, or putting out a fire in the kitchen, we're both going to end up frustrated. But I do want to hear about their lives. If your parents are busy, they may seem uninterested. Don't let your hurt feelings keep you from trying again.

Set A Time

If it's hard to get your parents to listen, set aside a few minutes every day when you can talk. For some families this might be mealtime. Others may find that bedtime or right after school works best. Most parents will be willing to set a time to talk with you. If you ask for it. If you do set a specific time to talk, protect that time. Take the phone off the hook, put the dog outside, turn off the TV, and eliminate any other distractions that could steal that time from you.

Make It Fun

Make that time as pleasant as possible. You may want to object to the way your parents have handled something; there may be privileges you want to ask for – if so, save it for later. Use this time to build lines of communication that will serve those other purposes later. Right now just open the door.

Be prepared – at first, you may be the one doing all the talking. As time goes on, your parents will learn to open up. You'll get some two-way communication going. But the key is to start talking to each other *regularly*. In many homes, the only time the children talk to their parents is when they're asking for something; the only time the parents talk to their kids is to scold them or tell them to do something. You will always need to ask your parents for privileges, but first you need to learn to just talk. Learn to talk to your parents, and you open the door for all kinds of growth and change.

Listen

Learn to listen. The best communication tool God gave you is not your lips – it's your ears. *Ask* your parents about themselves – about their lives, their jobs, their childhood, their frustrations, their plans, and hopes – and then listen.

One teenage girl discovered a new appreciation for her dad when she did this. At a church meeting, she had heard that it's important for fathers to spend time with their children, that fathers need to spend time alone with each child every day. The speaker suggested that they could go for a walk, or out to dinner, or just stay home and play a game.

But this girl's father had not done any of those things since she was a little girl, and she felt neglected. It seemed that all he did was work. She wondered whether he really loved her. So, after the church meeting, she asked him why they didn't spend more time together.

His answer changed their relationship. He told her, first, how much he wanted to be that kind of dad. For the first time, he explained how he wanted her to be able to go to college, and that the long hours he worked were providing the savings from which her college expenses would be paid. Her dad worked hard because he loved her and wanted to provide for her the things he had never had. Then he explained how guilty he had felt after hearing the message because he didn't have the time or energy to do the things the speaker had suggested.

Not all fathers have the courage or the communications skills to open up as this one did. But when they do, it's usually because of a simple question asked by someone they love – someone like you. Parents want to communicate with their children, but they don't know where to begin. If you're willing to ask the right questions and listen to the answers, you'll give them a place to start.

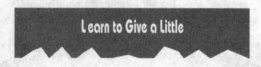

Learn to Give a Little

It's easy to approach your parents with tunnel vision. You know what you want, and that's all you see. Unfortunately, tunnel vision will make you totally unaware of the needs of your mother or father. And that's how many family arguments get started, with people screaming their demands at each other, blind to the needs of the others involved.

Here's the pattern. Let's say you want to go to the basketball game. So you approach your Dad.

Son: "Dad, can I have the car tonight to go to the basketball game?"

Dad: "No, I need the car to go to a trustee meeting tonight."

Son: "You have trustee meetings every night of the week. Why can't I have the car just once?"

Dad: "Because it's my car and I can do anything I want with it!"

And so on. In the first place, if all you want is to go to the game and all your father wants is to go to the trustee meeting, the argument need never start. But when you have tunnel vision and can't see the needs of the other person, it becomes impossible to see alternatives that would be acceptable to both parties. If you don't listen, all you hear is the word no. You then mistakenly assume that dad doesn't want you to go to the game, when all he really wants is to go to his meeting. If you argue, you'll back your dad into a corner that will make it difficult for him to make any decision in your favor.

So what *could* you do? There are lots of choices, really. Let's say your dad just said, "No, I need the car to go to a trustee meeting." Now's the time to use your communication skills to work out something mutually agreeable. Maybe you could offer to drop your dad off at his meeting and have someone else bring him home. If his meeting lasts long enough, you may be able to pick him up yourself. Even if that means that you have to leave the game a little early to get your dad, that's better than not going at all. Another option would be for you to catch a ride to the game with someone else. Or, as mortifying as it may sound, maybe your dad could drop you off at the game and you could get a ride back with one of your friends. If your real desire is to go to the game, the possibilities are many.

Of course, if your real desire is to have the car to yourself all evening, then the problem may be more difficult to solve. If that's the case, you should probably state it that way from the very start: "Dad, if it's possible I'd like to have the car tonight. Can we work that out?" Then your father might realize it is important for you to drive.

It's always important to keep these negotiations from dissolving into an argument. Even if you win the argument, in the long run you'll lose by alienating a parent. The next time, your mom or dad may say no just to prove they're still in control. Don't put them in that position. Learn to give a little – and do it without arguing. It will get you much further than insisting on having it all your way.

Cooperate

Cooperation works wonders. Think of the times, for instance, that you've asked for a privilege. When your parents said no, had they always thought through their answer? Not likely – saying no was simply the quickest and safest way to resolve the problem. So what's your best response? I'll give you a hint: The best response is not to ask "Why?" For some reason, that word is hard to say without it sounding like a challenge to your parents' authority. And, as you remember, a smart teenager will avoid such a challenge if he or she enjoys life.

You might instead put your question in a less threatening form: "Mom, can I explain why this is so important to me?" Or, "Could we take a minute to discuss this?" If, for instance, you want to go to a party, simply ask, "Mom, it's very important to me to be at the party tonight. Is there anything I can do that would make that possible?" If your parents still say no, they probably aren't going to change their minds. You'll have to accept their decision – gracefully, if you're wise. But at least the phrasing of this request gives them a chance to compromise. They may say, "If you promise you'll be home by twelve, you can go." Or "If you check to make sure the parents are home, you can go." Or "If you promise not to ride with that maniac Henry 'Hot Wheels' Wilson, you can go." Or "If you clean up your room first, you can go."

Parents don't like to be backed into a corner any more than you do. By allowing them to think through the possibilities, you give them the opportunity to find a solution that will allow you both to have what you want. Be careful to give them the respect and

99

consideration they need to keep such communication open. It's possible to manipulate and intimidate your parents into getting what you want – but that will only drive you further apart. Parents are not stupid. They know when they're being used.

Watch Your Words

The best intentions in the world can backfire if you use the wrong words. Here are some words and expressions that you should avoid when talking to your parents. These words cause parents to come apart at the seams. Some can make the veins in your father's neck bigger than your legs and cause you to be misunderstood. Others can hurt; they leave wounds that take a long time to heal.

Hate is a word that is rightfully banned from many homes. The words "I hate you" are like a knife through the heart. If you've used these words on your parents or other members of your family, ask them to forgive you and resolve never to use them again. God is crystal clear that the Christian's life should be characterized by love, not by hate.

Even if you have the privilege of openly expressing anger with your parents, try to do it in a manner that never brings into doubt your love for them. For example, instead of saying, "You make me angry," you should say, "Dad, when you say that, I feel angry." The difference is that the first way you're expressing displeasure with a *person;* the second way, you're expressing displeasure with an *action.* There's a big difference. If I say to you, "I can't stand you," you'll feel hurt. I'll have told you that your existence is unbearable to me. If, instead, I say to you, "I can't stand those kinds of actions," I'm expressing my distaste for something that you *do,* rather than for you as a person. And it's perfectly okay to express displeasure with a behavior. People can change their behavior. But they can't change the fact that they exist – at least, not in any acceptable way. If you express your disgust with a person, you attack his or her soul.

Be careful of your words. It pays to stop and think before you talk, especially when you're upset. Try to imagine, *before* you say them, what your words are going to sound like – because once those words pass your lips, they can never be taken back. I know of many relationships that have been damaged by words that never should have been spoken.

Cursing and vulgar language have no place in family communication. Even if other members of your family use these words when talking to each other, eliminate them from your vocabulary. In today's society, curse words are used so much that some people say they've lost their meaning. That may be true for the person who is insensitive enough to use them, but they never lose their meaning for those who are on the receiving end.

There are also phrases that, even though they aren't considered curses, serve only to hurt. "Drop dead," "Get lost," and "You make me sick," are words that destroy communication and people.

Remember this saying? "Sticks and stones may break my bones but names will never hurt me." If you were a robot, that saying might be true. But it's a lie. Broken bones heal after a time, but the hurt and pain from cruel words can last a lifetime. The tongue can be used to hurt or to heal. The power of the tongue is such that, according to Proverbs 25:15, "A gentle tongue can break a bone." In chapter 12:18 of the same book it says, "Reckless words pierce like a sword, but the tongue of the wise brings healing." Proverbs 10:19 says: "He who holds his tongue is wise." *Think* before you speak.

Another way to turn a parent into a fire-breathing dragon is to use words that drip with apathy – phrases such as "Okay, have it your way," "I don't care," "Big deal," and "So what?" Just last night, as I was in the middle of a disagreement with my daughter, she said, "Whatever," turned her nose in the air, and began to walk away. I think her first clue that I was upset was the sound of steam whistling through my ears.

"Get back here this very instant!" I screamed. Whenever a parent adds the words "this very instant" to any sentence, you know they

101

mean business. She came back faster than the Star Trek guys could have beamed her back.

"What's wrong?" she asked.

I explained, "If I'm in the middle of a disagreement with you, and you say, 'Whatever,' and walk away, the message to me is loud and clear: This discussion is not important enough to waste your time on. Maybe you mean it, maybe you don't; either way, no one wants to be treated like that." And, believe me, the parent who gets the "whatever" treatment is going to take it just that way.

"I don't care," is another apathy phrase. It means just what it says. Those words hurt when you are on the receiving end. Maybe you've felt the sting of that phrase when your parents used it on you. Maybe, as you argued for some privilege, your mother or father shouted in anger, "I don't care *what* you want!" Or, maybe, with a bored shrug of the shoulders, they said, "I don't care what you do." Either way, they seem to be saying, "You aren't worth the trouble to work this out, to negotiate a reasonable compromise." It even takes the joy out of getting whatever you were arguing for. We all want people to care.

Watch The Tone of Your Voice

Even the *way* we say words is important. Have you ever had your parents say, "Don't speak to me in that tone of voice!" They were talking about *how* you said the words.

Here's a little exercise you'll find fascinating. I'll show you how just changing the emphasis from word to word completely changes the meaning of a sentence – one that is repeated in hundreds of homes every single day: "I don't think you understand." Say this sentence out loud, putting a great deal of verbal emphasis on the word *I*. Expressed that way, the sentence implies that, although others may think you understand, *I* don't.

Now say the sentence again, only this time put the emphasis

on the word *don't*. Now the sentence implies that you have *tried* to communicate, but the information has not been understood.

Now emphasize the word *you*. If you use this sentence with your parents and emphasize the word *you,* you may not live to see another birthday. Say it out loud. It implies that the listener (in this case, your mother or father) is incapable of understanding. Emphasizing *you* changes a statement of fact into an insulting accusation. You might as well say, "I think you're stupid."

Emphasize the word *think* in this sentence, and you imply that you *believe* the listener doesn't understand, but that you're not sure.

Kind of amazing, isn't it? The same words take on different meaning, depending on how they're said. And it happens all the time. For instance: Your mom asks you how you liked the dinner she fixed, and you respond, "It's all right." There are a lot of ways to say, "It's all right." Say it wrong, and you might get the opportunity to eat your plate along with your meal. Say it right, and you'll probably get seconds on dessert.

It's easy to get careless with the tone of our communication. I've lost track of the number of times Diane has asked me, "Do you like this dress?" If I reply, "It's nice," she'll probably say, "I'll take it back – you don't like it." I *did* think it was nice, I *did* like it – but judging dresses is not one of my favorite pastimes. The lack of enthusiasm in my voice was misinterpreted to mean that I didn't like the dress. I've learned to pay careful attention when she shows me a dress. If I like it, I show enough enthusiasm to convince her. If I don't, I make little gagging sounds and then run for my life.

You'll sometimes find it necessary to go out of your way to make yourself understood.

Let Your Body Talk

If verbal communication can be easily misunderstood, you can imagine how easily *nonverbal* communication can be misunderstood.

After I gave my sister a mean look, my mother would say, "If looks could kill, your sister would be in heaven right now."

Under my breath I would respond, "If looks could kill, heaven is not the place she would be."

There are many nonverbal methods of communication that we use without even being aware of it. The raised eyebrow that says, "I don't understand." The wink that says, "I understand perfectly." Pay attention to your nonverbal communication – know what you're saying with your hands, your feet, your facial expression, and commit yourself to eliminating the negative nonverbal expressions from your life: stamping your feet, slamming doors, throwing things, looks that say "You're stupid," or "I hate you!"

Good communication doesn't come easily. It requires careful thought and a lot of practice. *Do everything you can to make it start happening.* Don't give up on this one. Between you and your parents there is a vital thread that can be used to build a loving relationship. That thread is communication. Build on it, make it strong, and protect it with all your energy.

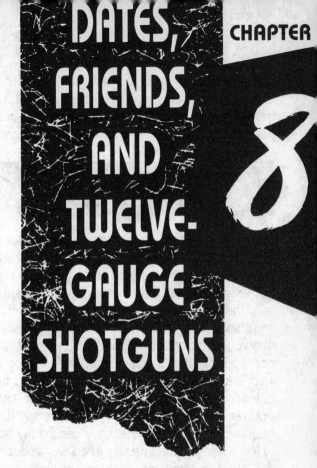

DATES, FRIENDS, AND TWELVE-GAUGE SHOTGUNS

Nothing has more potential for testing the relationship between a parent and a teenager than dating and friendships. Parents who never before interfered in your life suddenly take interest when you begin choosing your own friends. When you begin dating, they can seem like the KGB and CIA put together. You can make this a time to draw closer to your parents, or you can allow this time to drive you apart. The choice is yours.

Why do parents respond so strongly to your choices of friends and dating partners? Because of a few fears they have – four of them, in fact – that profoundly affect their attitudes about your dating. These fears are: fear of losing you, fear of the pain and destruction that can come with premarital sexual intimacy, fear of having you experience a broken heart, and fear of the devastation that comes from an ill-advised marriage. Because of the way our culture views maleness and femaleness, those fears are usually more intense with a daughter than they are with a son – but parents still feel these fears for their sons, and strongly.

THE FEAR OF LOSING YOU

Dating is one of the first major steps that take you away from your parents. For the first time, they see that your love is no longer theirs alone. I can tell you, from personal experience, that that's not easy to accept. Even though your parents may be happy for you, there's also a sadness that comes with the realization that you'll soon be gone. Most parents don't easily let go of someone they've spent years loving and protecting. Whether they show it or not, there will be an intense struggle raging inside your parents: They'll know that (eventually) you'll need to take that step toward independence, but they won't really want you to – and certainly not *yet*. Realize that, and try to understand. Some parents say, frequently and loudly, that they can hardly wait for their children to leave home. That's usually just a way of dealing with their sorrow that their children are growing up and away from them, but it causes their teenagers to wonder whether they really care.

If your parents seem to be fighting the inevitable truth that you're growing in independence, be grateful – even though their reluctance to grant your independence may cause problems for you. It's probably a sign of their love. As far as your mother and father are concerned, there is no person on the face of the earth who's worthy of you, and they're not about to share your love with someone who's less than perfect. Most teenagers get very angry when they sense this resistance. Instead, try accepting their feelings as a compliment. If they didn't love you, they wouldn't care if you were dating Dracula himself.

You may remember that, in the first chapter, I threatened to

SHE'S A NICE GIRL, BUT HER FATHER'S A LITTLE OVERPROTECTIVE.

Dates, Friends, and Twelve-Gauge Shotguns

shoot the first boy that came to our door to see my daughters. It's just that I thought the body lying there would serve as a deterrent. Other boys would see the body and decide she wasn't worth it. Okay, so maybe I won't *really* shoot anyone – but the strong protective impulse is still there.

Different parents respond differently to this ritual called dating, but the basic fear of losing you is there with all of them. This is where the communication lines discussed in the previous chapter will serve you well. It is vital at this period in your life that you reassure your parents of your love. They need to know now, more than ever, that you love them. If they are reassured of your love, there will be less of a sense of loss. Parents go through a kind of jealousy when you start dating. When they know you still love them, it's easier for them to accept the fact that, someday, you'll love someone else.

It's natural and necessary to move away from your parents, emotionally, during your teenage years. That process of moving away inevitably causes some tension at home. But it's a mistake to use dating (as many teenagers do) to escape those pressures. Those teenagers pull further away from their parents, making a difficult situation even worse. The further they distance themselves from their parents, the more emotional trauma their parents feel. The more emotional trauma they feel, the more they react. It can eventually lead to a total break in communication just when you need that communication most.

FEAR OF SEXUAL INTIMACY

Parents are also afraid that you'll become sexually intimate, and the pain that such intimacy can cause outside of marriage. They remember from personal experience the power of their own emotions. They may remember mistakes they made and the pain that accompanied those mistakes. They know the tremendous emotional and sexual pressure that can be a part of a dating relationship. In their effort to protect you, they may appear old-fashioned and unreasonable. And to make things worse, they find it extremely hard to talk about this fear. So, rather than discussing sex, they make rules.

It's as if there were an unexploded bomb that had landed in your neighborhood. Your parents were uncomfortable talking to you about the bomb, but they wanted to protect you from it. To keep you safe, they built a fence around the block where the bomb was. Of course, the fence also enclosed – and kept you away from – many other perfectly harmless areas of play, but it served its main purpose: It kept you safe. It also kept the bomb hidden and sufficiently far away so that it would not be necessary to discuss it. But that fence would have made you very angry, and because you had never discussed the bomb, you would be confused about why the fence was there in the first place.

Rather than experience the discomfort of talking about sexual responsibility, many parents simply build a fence. The fence is made of early curfews, lack of permission to attend events, and control over your social life. It's designed to keep you safe from the "bomb" and to keep you far enough from it to avoid uncomfortable discussion and confrontation.

What would make parents less inclined to set unrealistic boundaries? Their confidence in the standards you have set for yourself, and in your ability to live up to those standards under pressure. In other words, if they discover that you have built your own fence, they'll be less likely to build one for you.

But letting your parents know where you stand on these issues isn't easy. They avoid the subject because they feel inadequate and are unsure how to approach it, and they aren't likely to be too thrilled to hear *you* bring it up, either. So what can you do?

First, *watch for opportunities to tell your parents of your sexual beliefs and standards in nonthreatening ways.* Here's an example: When you watch television programs and movies together, you'll usually find ample opportunity to comment on the standards and situations portrayed on the screen and also to express where *you* stand. If your moral standards are high and you can communicate those standards to your parents, I guarantee you'll have a more relaxed parent the next time you go on a date. This kind of communication helps your parents see where you have built your own fence. If they know you have taken a stand and are willing to stick to it, they'll be more lenient.

This trust and openness can be continued if you allow your parents to be a part of your dating life. Now don't get me wrong – I'm not suggesting you take your parents with you on the next date. (Although that really isn't such a bad idea once in a while. Try it sometime.) What I am suggesting is that you share the joys and sorrows of dating with them. The smartest kids in the world are those who go directly to their parents' room after a date. If you take a little time to talk about the evening, they'll know what is going on and feel more secure in giving you freedom. If you felt that your date tried to compromise you in some way or was irresponsible, you lose nothing by letting them know. Think about it: If they've heard from your own lips that you were unwilling to put up with reckless driving or immoral behavior, they'll be much more at ease. They'll see that you have the maturity to make decisions on your own. On the other hand, if *you* have behaved in such a way that you can't tell your parents about it, then you can't expect them to be happy with your dating.

Even admitting your mistakes can increase their willingness to trust you. If they see that you can recognize and be dissatisfied with your own mistakes, they'll be more likely to trust your judgment. Considering the terrible things David did, I'm always amazed that God so dearly loved him. But read his story carefully in the Old Testament and you'll see that, in spite of the horrendous sins David committed, he didn't hide from God. Instead, he communicated with God and sought His forgiveness.

When my children have confessed some sin or admitted a mistake, I've never gloated in their confession. On the contrary, in spite of some sadness I have always been encouraged by their honesty and openness. It has always led me to trust them more.

So – if you haven't already done so, establish standards for your dating life and determine to stick to them. When dealing with the powerful impulses of love and sex, it is extremely important to have those standards in place *before* you get involved in a date or a close relationship. It's almost impossible to think rationally and make good decisions if you wait until you find yourself in a difficult situation.

Second, *and most important, always act responsibly when you are with someone of the opposite sex.* If you ignore friends and rudely shut the rest of the world out when you're with that special person, you won't be demonstrating to others how much you love your partner. Instead, you'll be demonstrating that you're not yet capable of responsible actions. I know it feels great to shut out the world and hang on to each other, but it doesn't feel great for the people you ignore. If you're careless in public, your parents will assume that you're even less sensible in private. Let your actions give them reason to trust you.

Even if you've communicated to your parents what your own sexual standards are, and they feel comfortable with them, all the good you've accomplished by that could be erased in an instant if your parents catch you tangled up with your boyfriend or girlfriend in a sweaty heavy-breathing contest. They've caught you inside your own fence, playing catch with the bomb. Demonstrate by your actions that you're not only responsible when others are around but also mature enough to act responsibly when you're alone.

THE FEAR OF A BROKEN HEART

Parents want to protect you from the pain of a broken heart. They won't be able to, of course – other than keeping you locked up all your life, there's nothing they can do to prevent it. You yourself can't guarantee it won't happen. But you can take steps to guard against unnecessary hurt, thereby assuring your concerned parents that you're not likely to die of heartbreak.

Learn to guard your heart. Don't fall head over heels in love with

111   Dates, Friends, and Twelve-Gauge Shotguns

every person that comes along. Rather than a string of intense love affairs, dating is supposed to be a string of great *friendships*. From this wide experience of getting to know a number of people well, you're supposed to be able to choose one person with whom to spend the rest of your life. If you show the maturity and common sense that allows you to have a lot of fun with a lot of people without getting emotionally and physically entangled in every relationship, you won't be hurt by every girl or boy that comes along.

Hurt and love go together. The only way you can avoid being hurt by love is to avoid love – something you probably don't want to do. But you can decide that your heart won't be up for grabs by just anybody. The more friendships you have with the opposite sex, the more sure you will be when you meet the "right one." And a nice fringe benefit is that your parents will see that you're smart enough to protect yourself. If you come home devastated every other week over broken relationships, they aren't going to be anxious to send you out there to get killed again. They'll look with suspicion on anyone who shows an interest in you. And you, too, will begin to think of relationships as negative experiences.

Back off and enjoy life. Enjoy great friendships instead of a series of high-risk, high-pain love affairs. When you find someone you really want to commit to, then you can decide to take the risk. Sure, you may experience several heartbreaks before you finally decide on a life partner. But you can keep them at a minimum by setting high standards and guarding your heart.

FEAR OF A POOR MARRIAGE

The last fear your parents face is that you will have to experience the suffering that comes with a poor marriage or a divorce.

The kind of people you choose as your friends and the kind of people you choose to date will determine the confidence your parents have in your ability to choose a good life partner. It's wise to include your parents in the evaluation of your friends and dates.

As a parent, I'm tempted to say that you should allow your parents to choose your friends for you. But I'm not stupid. Even though your parents would love to have that responsibility, you wouldn't stand still for it. And even if you did, you'd lose the chance to learn how to choose for yourself. No, you must choose your own friends. But your parents' evaluation of your friends and potential friends is a valuable tool you don't want to miss. They have in mind the very best for you. They can often foresee problems that you might overlook. As long as you're given the freedom to choose your friends, you shouldn't find it hard to listen to their opinions.

Make it a point to introduce your parents to *all* your friends. I insisted on it with Traci and Taryn, and at first they felt a little embarrassed by it. But they soon discovered that their friends liked it. They feel accepted at our home because we know each of them by name and we're aware of some of the problems they're facing. It's almost like an extended family for them. Although I don't impose myself on their activities, Traci and Taryn's friends know me well enough to know that I care about them. But none of that would have been possible except for one thing: Traci and Taryn's willingness to introduce their friends to me.

We talk often about the positive and negative aspects of the friends they choose. It's interesting to me that I'm rarely the one to make judgments. Both Traci and Taryn have exhibited an ability to have friends from a variety of backgrounds and to be objective in recognizing the qualities that make a good friend. That ability makes me much more relaxed about the friends they choose. Even if they choose to spend time with someone I don't totally approve of, they know why I don't approve and don't allow themselves to be negatively influenced.

If one of your friends refuses to meet your family, or if he or she tries to undermine your family relationships, that person isn't a friend at all. When one of the people you call a friend tries to get you to betray or deceive your parents, it's time to find new friends. Let people know that when someone attacks your family, they're attacking you. Allow your family to be friends with your friends.

The above suggestions work only on two conditions: **First,** *you must be mature enough to show that you aren't negatively affected by the people with whom you associate.* If you constantly demonstrate that you're pulled down by your friends, your parents are naturally going to try to make sure your friends are people who have higher standards than you. If, on the other hand, you have a wide variety of friends and are able to stand by your convictions, they will be less concerned about choosing your friends for you.

Second, *you must always communicate.* Go out of your way to let your parents know what you're thinking. You may not always want to follow their advice, but it's always wise to ask for it. And listen to them carefully – there may be a grain of truth there that could save you tremendous pain. Show them, by being open in your communication, that they can be confident of your maturity.

Marriage isn't a step to be taken lightly. If *they* know that *you* know that, and that you are thinking with your head as well as your heart, that will melt away a lot of their fear.

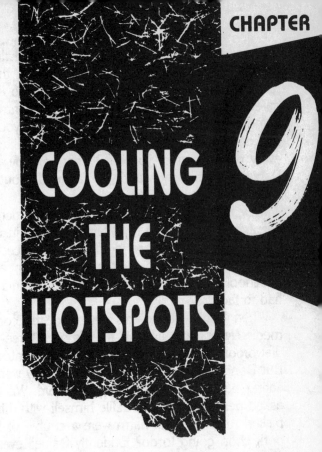

CHAPTER 9

COOLING THE HOTSPOTS

Most of the conflict in the average home starts over small things. You wouldn't believe the raging arguments that start because the toothpaste was squeezed from the wrong end, or a bed wasn't made, or a light was left on, or a door was left open. The arguments rarely start over big things like burning the house to the ground or hanging the cat.

When you reduce Christianity to its lowest common denominator, it's the way we respond to the little challenges of life that makes the difference. Bible heroes were men and women who were faithful in the little things. One of the greatest examples of that was Daniel, who was still a teenager when he first demonstrated his dedication to the Lord in the little things.

115

Imagine that some country attacked and defeated the United States. The leaders of that country ordered that all of the finest teenagers in the U.S. were to be brought to Asia to be indoctrinated in the customs of the conquering country. Can you imagine being one of those teenagers? Ripped from your home and family and deposited in the middle of a strange culture where you lived every day in fear of your life? That's exactly what happened to Daniel and his friends, and you can read about it in the first chapter of Daniel in your Bible.

Now, in the Bible story, the children were rich, handsome, intelligent, and came from royal families – but just because you use Stridex and Clearasil and don't drive a Mercedes or belong to a royal family, don't conclude that this story isn't about you. Your life at school and at home offers challenges much like those Daniel had to face.

When Daniel got to this new land, the conquering king immediately put him and his friends on a three-year aerobics and diet program, after which they were to go into the king's service. But Daniel recognized that the foods they were supposed to be eating had been forbidden by the Lord. Without hesitation, he asked permission not to defile himself with this food. What a nit picker! After all, what harm were a couple of french fries and a pork chop going to do? Evidently Daniel, even at this age, had already committed his life and his body to God. He wasn't about to go back on that commitment, even in the little things. In asking for special treatment, he was risking his life. But, because of Daniel's faithfulness in the little things, God honored him with great responsibility. He eventually became a trusted advisor to the king and his faith was known throughout the country.

Do you get discouraged in your attempts to live for Christ? Maybe it's because you keep looking for a big miracle to demonstrate your faith. Real faith is demonstrated in little things.

That's true around your house, too. The love you say you have for your parents will probably never require you to give your life for them. Right now the best way to demonstrate that love might be to make your bed or do your chores or set the table. Doesn't

sound very glamorous, does it? Yet the Christian faith is demonstrated best in little things like that.

Jesus emphasized that to Peter on several occasions. Peter was a lot like you and me – he wanted to please the Lord and was always talking about the big ways he was willing to do so. In John 13:37, Peter said to the Lord, "I will lay down my life for you!"

Jesus responded, "Will you really lay down your life for me? I tell you the truth, before the rooster crows, you will disown me three times!"

How could Peter say he would *die* for Christ if he couldn't even *live* for Him? How could he expect to give his life for the Lord when he was not willing to admit to a little servant girl that he knew who Christ was? True to Jesus' prediction, that night when Peter was asked if he was one of the disciples, he cursed and denied that he even knew Christ. Not just once, but three times! Peter demonstrated that his commitment to die for Christ was empty. The words "I love you" take on full expression only in your behavior. You demonstrate your love for your parents in the little things of everyday life.

That was graphically illustrated to me one day when I decided to vacuum the house for my wife. I was sitting in the house with nothing to do when the vacuum caught my eye. I hadn't touched the machine for years, but it looked lonely, so I decided to play with it. First I vacuumed the living room. I noticed that the nap of the rug took on different hues, depending on the direction I was vacuuming. In the living room, I made wonderful stripes. In the family room, I experimented by going both ways and ended up with a beautiful checkerboard pattern. I got so carried away I vacuumed the whole house. I was just getting ready to call the neighbors and offer to do their rugs when Diane came home.

She walked in, came to a screeching halt, and stood with her mouth open. First she looked at the beautifully vacuumed rugs, then she looked at me. A huge smile formed on her lips, she dropped everything in her hands, and attacked me. She gave me a million kisses with such energy we broke a coffee table. It was wonderful! I suppose I had tried dozens of times to get her to act that way by saying sweet things like, "I love you, and I think you are beautiful, now give me a million kisses." My words evidently couldn't convince her. Simply vacuuming the rug (luckily, she didn't know I'd had fun doing it) did what all the words in the world could not do. When it comes to love, actions speak louder than words.

The sources of frustration and conflict in most homes revolve around a fairly standard set of circumstances: the condition of your room, the distribution and completion of family responsibilities (chores), homework, your personal schedule, and the establishment and enforcement of rules and regulations. Learn to look at those areas of conflict differently; they're also the areas that will give you opportunity to express love to your parents. This is where the rubber meets the road. How you respond to the conflict generated here, and how much you are willing to work toward pleasing your parents in these everyday experiences, will indicate the depth of your desire to love your mom and dad.

THE DISASTER AREA

Let's start with your room. Personally, I believe that your room is not a direct reflection on you or your family. If you have a messy room, you won't be condemned to live another life somewhere as a pig, as I was once told. I've met many people who had terrible rooms and turned out to be wonderful people. I meet one of these people every morning when I look in the mirror. I've always had a hard time keeping a neat room and I probably always will.

So if your room looks like a disaster area, take heart. There is no place in Scripture where it says, "God turneth his back on those that haveth rooms that looketh as though a hurricane hath wreckethed them." But that doesn't give you an excuse to stop trying. Even though the condition of your room doesn't affect your personal worth, for some strange reason it affects your parent's attitude. Although it's a struggle for me to keep my *own* room neat, I continue to expect my children to keep theirs neat.

About a month ago I announced that I was going to go through Taryn's room and throw away anything I found lying on the floor – an empty threat, since there are no dump trucks large enough to carry such a load. It was also an empty threat because I don't have the courage to search her room thoroughly. She likes to collect bugs, snakes, snails, spiders, and anything else that will hold still long enough for her to pounce on it. After running into two living things (I didn't stop to find out what they were) and one dead thing, I gave up the project. I just hung a sign on the door that said, "Keep America beautiful – nuke this room."

I was only half joking. I find myself very intolerant of having my child's room in this condition. We've had many conflicts trying to solve this problem. Then Taryn discovered a secret that might be helpful to you. If you clean up your room without being asked, it makes your parents very very happy. She does this on occasion just to freak me out. Take advantage of this to make your parents happy often.

But when I *ask* her to clean her room, she wails, "But it'll take all day!" Yes, it might take all day – the first time. After that, take the time to put things away as you use them, and the room will stay clean. Put up a sign for yourself that says, "Hang it up." That'll remind you not to throw that dress or coat on the floor. You have to hang it up sometime, so why not let it be now? Then you won't have to look for it under a truckload of other garbage.

Put up another sign where you'll see it as soon as you get out of bed: "I can make it!" Then, when you crawl out of bed, prove to yourself that you can really make it by turning around and making it.

You have to admit it feels good to leave a clean room in the morning. It feels even better to come back to a clean room after school. You can't imagine how good your parents feel when they look at a clean room. If it makes them happy and avoids hassles, why not make the effort to keep it clean?

A lot of the drudgery can be alleviated by making it fun. The signs are just a beginning. Compete with yourself to see how long you can go without trashing your room. When you finally leave the place in a mess, start over and try to break your old record. Find a friend who's crazy enough to compete with you; set it up like a disarmament treaty between the United States and the Soviet Union. Arrange for "on-site" inspections, spy on each other – the whole works. The key is to make it fun. Before you know it, keeping your room clean will become a habit. Then you can move on to other environmental issues, like saving the poor animals my daughter collects in her room.

CHORES

Another conflict in most families is the responsibility for doing chores.

A family is like a team. That team will function most efficiently if all the members work together and are willing to pull their share of the load. It's easy to look at your parents as the ones who should do all the work so that you're free to enjoy life. After all, no one enjoys dishes, laundry, or garbage detail. Not even your parents – especially after they've finished a full day of work at their job. Most parents are enthusiastically grateful if you're willing to take some of the load from their shoulders. Look around – see what needs to be done, and then do it without being asked. That'll blow a parent away. It demonstrates your willingness to be a part of the team and your ability to accept responsibility. Sit down with your parents and list the jobs that are necessary to make your home run smoothly. That willing attitude may lead you and your parents to some creative ways to share those tasks.

Think ahead to eliminate problems in completing your chores. If your job is to mow the lawn and you know you want to be gone this coming Saturday, don't wait until Saturday morning and then try to get out of it. If you do, and if your parents insist that you stay to do your chores, you'll think they're being unfair – but the conflict could have been avoided if you'd planned ahead.

121

If you want to be gone on Saturday, plan to mow the lawn Friday after school. If on Wednesdays you're in charge of garbage detail, and the garbage is overflowing Tuesday night, don't wait until Wednesday to empty it.

Even if you run across work that is someone else's responsibility, if it needs doing, do it! The other night the living room was more cluttered than usual. Even the dogs were afraid to walk through for fear of getting lost. I asked one of the girls to please help clean it up. When I returned a few minutes later, it was still a terrible mess.

"Didn't I ask you to clean up this room?" I asked.

"I did," she answered. "At least, I picked up my stuff. The rest of it belongs to somebody else. It's not my job."

I quietly explained (okay, so maybe it wasn't quietly) that if we all operated that way the family would never survive. It's easy to rationalize that the only fair chores are those that benefit you personally. But what if your father and mother only shopped for the food *they* ate? What would happen if they spent their earnings only on themselves and refused to help with *your* clothes, food, and education?

Being part of a family really does require teamwork. It's tempting to think of yourself as the center of the world and to believe that everything else exists to serve your needs. Frankly, I often slip into that mode of thinking myself. But if every member of a family had that attitude, the result would be disaster. It takes only one person to break that terrible pattern. That's why you will benefit from having a loving and giving attitude toward your parents. When you allow God to help you consider the needs of others before your own, you'll find that they respond in the same way, and that there are other people looking out for *your* happiness. This doesn't happen overnight, of course. You may have to begin acting with compassion before you *feel* like it, and it may be awhile before the others in your family pick up on your example.

Paul says, "Love must be sincere. Hate what is evil; cling to what is good. Be devoted to one another in brotherly love. Honor one another above yourselves" (Romans 12:9-10). Go beyond the call of duty. An extra few minutes a day is all it takes to make everyone's load a little lighter.

Do your work with pride. Give every job you tackle your best shot. As a teenager, I was responsible for mowing the lawn. Since my father had a yard that covered half the state of Minnesota, I hated this job with a passion. And it showed in my work, too, because when I was finished the lawn always had a punk hairstyle. One year, while on vacation, we drove past a mansion with a beautifully manicured lawn. The wheel tracks from the lawnmower were in ruler-straight lines. In fact, the caretaker of this lawn had mowed it twice; the second time, he mowed at an angle so that the lawn had a beautiful diamond pattern to it. (Maybe that's where I got the idea for vacuuming the rug at different angles.)

From that day, I always tried to mow *our* lawn with absolutely straight lines. It became a challenge. Before I knew what was happening, I found myself enjoying that job. Not that I looked forward to it, but at least it was no longer the dreary task it had been.

Make your bed as neatly as possible; empty the garbage in record time; clean your room until people are afraid to enter because they think it's a holy place. Follow these simple rules, and the hassles will decrease, more will get done, your parents will be happier, and you will be demonstrating the love of Christ in the ways it was meant to be demonstrated.

YOUR SCHEDULE

One of the hot spots of conflict often overlooked is your schedule. Parents have a way of getting upset when they see a teenager busy every night of the week, partly because of their own fears and insecurities and they would like to spend time with you. Taking a few simple steps will make this less of a problem.

First, *leave time in your schedule for your family.* If you plan time at home, your parents won't be so reluctant to allow you time away. If, on the other hand, you're suddenly no longer available as a member of the family, your parents might be scared into keeping you at home.

Second, *give your family advance notice of your schedule,* especially if you need their help getting to and from events. Sure, there are times when special events come up at the last minute, but you'll find (if you haven't already) that parents resist last-minute surprises. The more advance notice they have, the less hassles you'll face. (But don't forget to gently remind them as time goes along, because parents also have notoriously short memories.)

Third, *make your schedule known in the form of a request rather than a demand.* Rather than saying, "These are the things I'm going to do next week," try saying, "Here are some of the events I'd like to attend next week, Mom — do you see any conflicts?"

HOMEWORK

Be sure to make your homework an important part of your schedule. In fact, it should be the *first* item on your schedule. Putting it off will only cause it to get in the way. Have a quiet, clean little hermit corner where you can work. If it isn't clean, then clean it up. If it isn't quiet, you might want to wear ear plugs or even study in the library. Many college students do most of their studying in the library. Regardless of where you choose to study, start on homework as soon as you can and keep at it until it's done. There may be nights that your homework keeps you from going out, but that's a small price to pay compared to what happens if you put it off and get behind. And you'll avoid a lot of arguments with your parents if you take the initiative to get your homework done without being asked.

Summing up: The secret to avoiding stress over your room, your chores, your schedule, and your homework is to be willing to live with others in mind — to be the one who is first willing to change and do whatever it takes to make living at home a blessing rather than a curse. That *sounds* simple, but it's hard to do, mainly because it requires action on your part.

At the beginning of this chapter I advised you not to look for big miracle ways to demonstrate your love. This chapter has talked about some of the little ways to show love. Likewise, don't expect big miracles as a result of your actions. In fact, you may even think that no one has noticed what you've been trying to do. Even so, there *is* a miracle going on – and that miracle is what's happening inside your own heart. It's true that it's hard to keep on loving when the people you're expressing your love for aren't responding, but it's been done before – and with God's help, you can find the courage and strength to do it in your family.

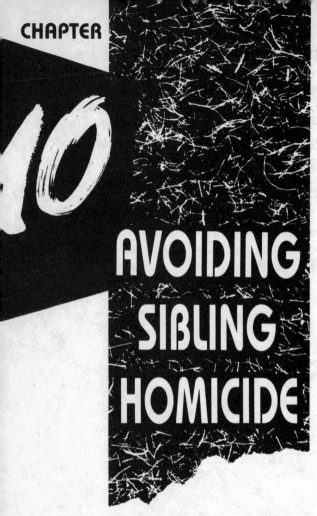

CHAPTER

10

AVOIDING SIBLING HOMICIDE

Sibling rivalry (warfare among brothers and sisters) has existed since the beginning of the human race. In fact, big-league fighting started with the very first family. The first two brothers on the face of the earth ended their relationship when one of them killed the other (Genesis 4). When God didn't accept Cain's offering, Cain grew so angry and jealous that he enticed his brother into a field where he killed him. Before your eyes brighten because this is an option you've never considered, you should be aware that God was not pleased with Cain's behavior.

Jealousy drove Joseph's brothers to sell him as a slave. We're not talking here about a punch in the eye or a verbal attack. These guys were deadly serious. They had planned to kill Joseph. God wasn't very happy with their actions either.

All of that was thousands of years ago, but some things haven't changed – intense, negative feelings still frequently surface among brothers and sisters. Many teenagers still find cruel and unusual ways of working out their aggressions and hostility on their siblings. This chapter can't stop all the fighting in your family, but it can help you cope with your feelings and teach you how to work out your differences without staining the carpets with blood.

KNOW WHY YOU FIGHT

One of the most annoying and difficult aspects of teenage living is dealing with brothers and sisters. How is it possible to feel so many conflicting emotions toward another person? Is it wrong to have these feelings? What should you do about how you feel?

Here are some of the reasons sibling relationships are so difficult during the teen years:

1. As a teenager, you're very sensitive about personal injustice, self-worth, independence, privacy, and love. One of the greatest obstacles and threats to all the above is your brother or sister.

2. Just when you're hoping to be treated with special respect, a younger brother or sister may be treated with outright favoritism. While you're in constant trouble with your parents, it seems as though that wicked brother or sister gets away with everything.

3. Your siblings are aware of all your weaknesses, and the rats don't miss one opportunity to use those weaknesses to their advantage. When you most need a sense of self-worth and respect, a brother or sister will not hesitate to call you a worm or a cockroach, which makes you feel like a worm or a cockroach.

4. These subhuman creatures give you absolutely no privacy and have no respect for your belongings. They borrow without

Avoiding Sibling Homicide

asking and break, mutilate, or lose some of your most important possessions. They know what you value most and put those things at the top of their hit list. They listen in on phone conversations, enter the most holy places in your room without asking, and have no idea what it means to keep a secret.

5. Sometimes it seems as though your parents conceived them just to spy on you. They're like a miniature KGB. Just when you think you can trust them (what a laugh), they tell what you did last week and get you grounded for the next three years. And as your parents pronounce your punishment, an ever-so-faint smile plays across your siblings' lips. Oh, if you could just get your hands on those lips.

6. If it's a younger brother or sister, they have an uncanny ability to know when you want to be alone with your friends and con your parents into making you take them along. Better yet, they prove themselves so infantile that your parents make you stay home to babysit.

7. Older brothers or sisters seem to be intent on leaving you out of their lives, ashamed that you even exist.

My teenage friends have wondered out loud if God perhaps put their brothers and sisters on earth just to make them suffer, kind of like the way He tested Job in the Bible. When God offers no answer to that question, the next one is, "Why do they treat me this way?"

They treat you that way for the same reasons you hate to be treated that way. For example, that younger brother who is always tagging along threatens the sense of independent identity you want to establish with your friends. Yet it's that same search for identity that makes him want to go with you. He's not trying to ruin your good time – he just wants to be with you. Being with you gives him importance. He admires you because of the freedom you have. To him, you're a hero (even though he may not always talk like it). But *you* know that his presence will destroy your evening, so you assume that's why he wants to come in the first place. You have individual needs; so does your brother. It's natural to try to fulfill those needs. Trying to fulfill them in a family setting will almost always infringe on the needs and rights of other members of the family, causing friction. The little sister wants to feel grown up, so she sneaks into the big sister's room to try on all her clothes. The big sister wants to feel like an adult, so she resents any unauthorized intrusion into her room. Unless somebody tries to understand why these things are happening, it's a standoff.

Another reason brothers and sisters treat each other the way they do is that siblings serve as a kind of punching bag for emotions that can't be released on anyone else. Your sister, when she gets a royal chewing out from your parents, can't lash back at them. She can't take it out on her friends. But she wants to scream at somebody in the worst way – and at that moment you walk into the room, whistling. You're probably going to be told to keep your stupid bird talk to yourself. You've become the safety valve through which she can vent her emotions. And if you keep it up, or tease her, or just in general give her a bad time, you'd better not let her get her hands on you.

Your brother has just suffered humiliation at the hands of some bullies at school. He wanted to fight back like the karate kid, but he didn't want the family to have to scrape him up off the sidewalk. What's he going to do with all that anger? Where can he release it that won't cost him a black eye or a month without the use of the car? If you're nearby, you may be the answer to his prayers. Only with the people you love can you safely vent your frustrations, because deep down you know that, when it's all over, they'll still stand by you. After all, they *have* to love you – you're part of the family.

To make things worse, parents tend to treat children with varying degrees of favoritism and discipline. They also have a habit of comparing children with each other in an effort to motivate them. If you tell your parents that, they'll probably deny it. And in fact, they don't love one child more than the other – but they do treat each of you differently. Older children are allowed more freedom just because they're older. A child who has a good sense of responsibility will be given more privileges than one who is irresponsible. No matter how rational such preferential treatment

Avoiding Sibling Homicide

seems to your parents, if you're the younger or less responsible child it won't seem fair to you. If you tell your parents – gently – how this kind of treatment makes you feel, they might be willing to make adjustments. But it's more likely that they'll feel justified in their actions and will continue. Your solution? Take it out on your brother or sister who's getting privileges that you aren't. It's hard to love someone who's getting special treatment when you feel you're being treated unfairly.

If you live in a family and bleed when you cut yourself, then you'll struggle with brothers and sisters. There'll be times when you'd like to sell them to the nearest pet shop. Unless you're superhuman, you won't always feel a mushy loving feeling toward the other kids in your house. You have to compete with them for the affection of your parents, you have to live up to standards they've set, you have to share your privacy and even your most important stuff with them. You'll often find yourself feeling frustration and anger toward these other humans that you know you love. Should you feel guilty? No. These feelings and frustrations are common to every family. Should you lure your brother and sister into a field somewhere and fix 'em good? Of course not. God has made it clear that He's not pleased with that kind of solution. *Then what can I do?* you ask.

KNOW HOW TO FIGHT

I'm glad you asked. There's no magic formula that will put an end to all the fighting in your home, but there are some ground rules that can keep the conflicts from escalating into an all-out war.

First, it's important for you to know that your relationship with your brothers and sisters will have a direct effect on your relationship with your mother and father. Few things can cause a parent to become a raving maniac quicker than constant bickering and fighting among the kids – and I speak from experience. If you

learn to control your fighting with your brothers and sisters, you'll notice a change in your parents. The glassy gaze and the dark circles beneath your parents' eyes will disappear. Their voices will become much quieter, and they won't foam at the mouth as often.

Here are the ground rules that will keep your parents sane and keep you alive.

1. Don't always run to your parents with every little conflict. You can avoid a lot of hard feelings and add years to your parents' lives by learning to fight your own battles. Sit down with your brothers and sisters and lay out ground rules for settling conflicts.

2. When a problem comes up, have a cooling-off period. Give each other time to calm down and think about what alternatives might help settle the issue. Then, when you come together, agree not to blame each other. Deciding whose fault it is settles nothing. Concentrate on solving the problem.

3. Don't get into a name-calling contest. Agree to talk about your feelings and the problem instead of arguing about the kind of slimy creature the other person reminds you of. Don't use profanity or insults – that only leads to more anger and hides the solution. I have seen kids fight for so long that they forgot the original problem. All of the cruel rhetoric only served to cause anger and hatred.

4. Avoid physical abuse. There is never an excuse to physically attack your brother or sister. If they use physical abuse, defend yourself by getting away, not by fighting back; if you do, they'll soon lose interest because it will have ceased to be fun. When you fight back, unless you have a powerful right hook, you're encouraging it to happen again.

5. Be a peacemaker. Learn to say, "I'm sorry." My mother and father used to have a saying that I absolutely detested. When my sister and I were trying to fix the blame on each other, they would say, "It takes two to fight." As much as I disliked being told this, I've discovered that it's absolutely true. And that's good news, because it means that *you* can make a difference, even if your brothers and sisters are unwilling to change. It does take two to fight, and if you refuse to fight there can't *be* a fight. Nothing is more unsatisfying than fighting with someone who doesn't fight back – except maybe fighting with someone who loves you back. If you refuse to fight, you will see a marked difference in the tension and conflicts in your home.

6. Avoid scorekeeping. There's a real temptation to keep a private score of all the times you've been wronged or have given in. Then when your patience has worn so thin you could drive a truck through it, you announce the score: "I gave in last time – it's your turn for once." "This is the third time I've forgiven you, and I refuse to do it any more until you change." God doesn't put limits on our love. As difficult as it may sound, we need to keep on loving and forgiving, even when we aren't getting the same treatment in return.

7. Find outlets for your anger. You might ask, "What should I do when I feel like drop-kicking my brother clear off the planet?" The answer is, "Kick something else instead." Don't get me wrong – I'm not suggesting you should find a cat or dog or any other living creature. Rather than drop-kicking your brother or the family cat, take a quick walk, throw some rocks in a safe direction, or beat up the sidewalk with a big stick. It doesn't even have to be a physically aggressive action; playing a musical instrument can work. As a teenager, when I would get angry with someone I would retreat to my room and play my guitar. Before long, I wouldn't feel angry anymore. Maybe that wouldn't work for you; you must find your own release for anger. Find something that helps you, and then use it as a safety valve.

8. Avoid stupid arguments. Don't let yourself get bent out of shape over nothing. Some arguments children have are so ridiculous they're funny: "Dad, she's looking at me!" "I was thinking about playing with that first!" "This is my side of the house!" "You started it!" But carry those arguments into the teen years and they cease to be funny. They become the kinds of arguments that drive parents crazy. They are the arguments of children; they have no place in the life of a mature teenager.

These suggestions point out how to fight fair and settle conflicts in a way that causes as little harm as possible to your brother or sister. But there's another step the Christian teenager should be willing to take: Begin learning how to avoid conflicts in the first place.

KNOW HOW TO AVOID FIGHTING

Although feelings of conflict and frustration will accompany any relationship, those feelings don't have to result in open warfare. It's possible to deal with the problems that arise between brothers and sisters without constant physical or verbal battles. If you're a Christian, you definitely have a responsibility to make every effort to resolve conflicts in a peaceful manner and avoid them whenever possible. Here are some suggestions that might help you do that.

1. Learn to live for others. I have, on occasion, run across families that have managed to live relatively peacefully under difficult circumstances. In each of these families, the thread that held them together had nothing to do with economics or social status – it was a sense of unity and a genuine caring for each other.

It's so easy to think that the world revolves around you. That everything on the earth, including your family, was put here so that your needs could be met. The common denominator in each of those peaceful families was the absence of that kind of thinking. The individual members of the family were thinking about the needs of the others in the family.

A brother and sister in Seattle, Washington, amazed me with the love they demonstrated for each other. While staying in their home, I was delighted to see the older brother wake his sister in the morning and ask what she would like for breakfast. Instead of the cruel way a brother often treats his sister, he treated her with the kindness that is usually only reserved for a very close friend. She treated him with respect and admiration and proudly told me of his athletic accomplishments. When they each left the house that morning to go their separate ways it was with expressions of love and good luck. Compare that attitude with the fighting that usually rings through a house before school. An unselfish view of life, backed by an all-out effort to care for the other members of your family, can make a miraculous difference in your home.

2. Respect the privacy of your brothers and sisters. Everyone in your family, including you, needs a space of his own. It's easy for resentment to build when another person continually invades that space. If you have separate rooms, be sure you knock before you enter someone else's room. If you sleep in the same room, establish drawers or closets that can be privately yours. Then respect the privacy of those areas. The greatest single cause of fights in the home is the invasion of personal privacy. Respect the privacy of others, and you'll eliminate much conflict.

3. Respect their property. No matter how agreeable you think your brother or sister might be, never borrow anything without asking. To do so is an infringement on privacy. When you do get permission to borrow something, care for it as though it were your own. Some of the loudest arguments I hear are the result of one child's borrowing the property of another and then destroying it.

4. Learn to give a little. If there's an activity both of you want to attend, but one of you has to stay home to babysit, why not occasionally offer to stay home so your brother or sister can go? I've seen many fights that started with this kind of conflict end with angry parents insisting that *both* stay home. Which, of course, leaves us with two teenagers sitting home blaming each other for the boring evening and taking their anger out on the poor child they were forced to babysit. The best solution to the problem would have been for one of the teenagers to offer to babysit in the first place, avoiding the argument, avoiding their parents' anger, and increasing their chances to be given future privileges in response to their cooperative attitude.

There's nothing you can do to force anyone else to give in. So why not let it be you? If you really care about the others in your family, then you should be willing to occasionally suffer some inconvenience for their good. It's amazing how quickly things begin to change when just one person is willing to demonstrate the unconditional love of Christ. If your sister comes home anxious over a test she must take the next day, you could offer to set the table and do the dishes, even if it isn't your turn. What should you expect in return? Nothing. Eventually she may thank you and offer to reciprocate – but if you expect it, you may be disappointed. Help her simply because she needs your help.

5. Stick up for your brothers and sisters. Even though you undoubtedly have disagreements with your brothers and sisters at home, it's very important to always stick up for them outside the family. One of the most cruel things you can do is join with your friends in teasing or berating some member of your family. We all need to have a safe place to call home, a place where we know we are protected and loved. It may be okay to fight among ourselves once in awhile, but it's vital that your brothers and sisters know that you'll defend them against the attacks that come from outside. Let your family know that you're on their side. Be protective; never allow someone to con you into taking a stand against the ones you love.

6. Don't tease. I have watched teenagers tease younger brothers or sisters until they cried for mercy. I have also seen younger children use the imaginary safety of their young age to pester older siblings beyond the breaking point.

After seeing a boy in my youth group tease his younger sister cruelly one day, I grabbed him by the arm and began to lecture him. He cursed me and told me it was none of my business.

"Her sadness *is* my business," I said. "Look at her!"

She was sitting in a corner, weeping uncontrollably. Looking up, she saw through her tears the grip I had on her brother's arm. (It was probably turning blue.) Without hesitation, she leaped from her corner and attacked *me!* She thought I was hurting her brother, and she came to the rescue like a mother bear protecting her cubs.

The boy stood there with his mouth open. I think he realized for the first time that he was not just teasing this little person – he was hurting her. And she was not just any little person; she was his sister who loved him and was willing to endanger herself trying to protect him. As we talked it became evident that teasing was like a game to him. He constantly teased because he loved to see her emotional reaction. But when he realized how much his teasing hurt her, his behavior began to change. Oh, he still teases her. It's evidently one of the requirements of being a brother. But now he knows when to quit, and his teasing is gentle.

7. Be willing to share. This point speaks for itself. A willingness to allow your brothers and sisters to use your "stuff" takes away the basis for a tremendous amount of fighting.

8. Avoid tattling. Tattling on other members of the family builds a great amount of resentment and mistrust. Try to work out your problems among yourselves. Go to your parents only when you agree to do so because you can't reach an agreement by yourselves. Your parents will be much more willing to arbitrate some problem you have worked on together than to listen as you tattle and blame each other. If you know your brothers or sisters are doing something wrong, talk to *them* about it. Your job is not to accuse or try to solve the problem, but just to let them know you care. Yes, they'll probably tell you to get lost – but if you continually respond in love, sooner or later that love is going to get through.

9. Pray for your brothers and sisters. If possible, try to find time to pray *with* them as well. In one family, the children have one time each week when they sit together and share their needs, fears, and blessings. If they feel any resentment toward each other, they use this time to talk about it. Then they pray for each other. During this time it isn't unusual to hear them ask each other for forgiveness or ask God to help each other.

Obviously, it isn't going to be easy to develop this kind of openness with your brothers and sisters. But it's worth every effort you can muster. When people come with open hearts before God, their spirits are molded together. If you're the only one in your family who cares enough to even approach God, then make a

Avoiding Sibling Homicide

habit of praying for your brothers and sisters. Pray that God will help them with the problems that they face and that He will continue to help you show His love to them. Prayer is a powerful tool – not only because of God's ability to answer your prayers, but also because of the way it cleanses your own heart.

I can almost guarantee that, if you'll observe the suggestions in this chapter, the bickering and fighting in your family will be cut in half. Adhering to them will take away the reasons you fight in the first place. It will not be easy. But the peace and love that will come to your family will make it well worth the effort.

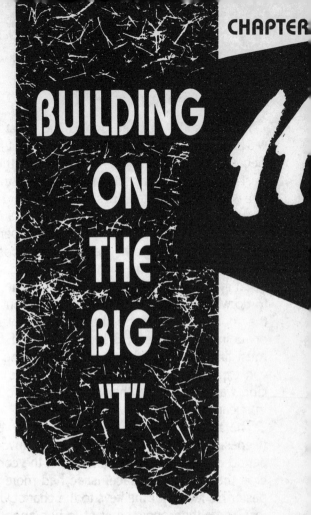

CHAPTER

BUILDING ON THE BIG "T"

11

The big "T" stands for trust. If your family knows they can trust you, those last years you spend at home will be enjoyable years that you long remember. But building trust isn't easy; it takes time and careful attention to detail. Once built, it's like a fragile piece of glass – it can be broken in a single careless moment. But it's worth the effort to build and maintain trust because it opens up a whole world of responsibility and opportunity that you otherwise wouldn't have. This chapter will show you how to build and maintain a solid base of trust.

Your personal trust in God is the most solid foundation on which to build trust with others. Why is that foundation essential? Because it's the foundation upon which the whole *meaning* of trust is built. In other words, God provides the perfect example of one who can be trusted. He sets the standard from which to build.

Many times I've heard people say, "I can't even trust myself." And that's true. You must have a more dependable standard than just satisfying your own desires. The apostle Paul realized he couldn't depend on his own flesh. He said, "I know that nothing good lives in me, that is, in my sinful nature. For I have the desire to do what is good, but I cannot carry it out. For what I do is not the good I want to do; no, the evil I do not want to do – this I keep on doing" (Romans 7:18-19). Because of our sinful nature, we must first trust God; that trust in Him is the base from which we can expect to be trusted. If it's your desire to be everything that God wants you to be, then you have the foundation upon which trust can be built.

The story of Abraham and Isaac is a powerful example of trust (Genesis 22). Even though the people involved lived in another period of history, they faced many of the conflicts you do. By the time the story takes place, Isaac had more than likely started to pester his father for the keys to the chariot. Just like you, I'm sure that, more than once, he went to bed angry with his dad. But it's obvious that a special trust existed between Isaac and his father. It was so strong that they could trust each other with their very lives.

One night Abraham was suddenly awakened by the Lord Himself. God asked him to do something that must have seemed very bizarre: "Take your son, your only son, Isaac, whom you love, and go to the region of Moriah. Sacrifice him there as a burnt offering on one of the mountains I will tell you about" (Genesis 22:2).

What was Abraham thinking when God said that? First of all, Abraham knew that God would not allow his son's life to come to a permanent end because God had given him the greatest promise that a father of that day could receive. He had promised that Isaac would be the father of many generations, and that from those descendants would come the Messiah. Now, as he lay in the darkness, God was asking him to sacrifice this son, even though Isaac had never been married or had children. I'd have been tempted to remind God of His promise and suggest that He wasn't being fair. But Abraham simply obeyed God.

As soon as morning came, he saddled a donkey, gathered some wood, and took some of the hired help with him to the mountains. Although it was clear to Isaac that his father was following a directive from God, he evidently didn't know exactly what it was. He did know there was going to be a sacrifice. Halfway up the mountain, he revealed his concern: "Father? ... The fire and wood are here ... but where is the lamb for the burnt offering?" (Genesis 22:7).

Without hesitation, his father replied, "God himself will provide the lamb for the burnt offering, my son" (Genesis 22:8).

Now assume for a moment that you're Isaac. If you hadn't already figured out that things were going to get a little hot, you'd certainly catch on when your father laid you on the altar and reached for the matches. Yet the Bible shows no record of a struggle. This father and son trusted each other completely. Isaac was at his father's mercy. It appeared that his father intended to kill him, yet he didn't resist. And consider this: Abraham also showed tremendous trust in his son. Remember that Abraham was over a hundred years old by this time – he could have easily been overpowered by Isaac. If Abraham hadn't trusted his son, he could have had the servants jump him at the bottom of the mountain, tie him up, and carry him helpless to the place of sacrifice. Instead, they left the servants behind and went on together. I'm sure there must have been some fear and confusion in their minds, but their trust held firm. And, as Abraham raised the knife to take his son's life, God intervened and spared Isaac. Then He provided a lamb for the sacrifice just as Abraham had said He would. With great thanksgiving, and with a renewed trust in God and each other, they sacrificed the lamb to Him.

You're probably shaking your head and laughing to yourself, "Isaac was crazy – his dad was trying to kill him! How could he go on trusting him when he realized what was going on?" Isaac trusted his father because he was convinced that he was following the command of God. No doubt on many occasions Abraham sat with Isaac and told him of God's wonderful promise and the special part he played in that promise. Through the years, Isaac had seen the complete faith his father had in God. He knew that his own birth had come at a time when his parents were no longer capable of having children because of their old age. He had seen his father obey God without question time and time again. Never had Isaac seen God let his father down, and he knew that God would not go back on His word now.

Because his father trusted God, Isaac trusted his father.

Hebrews 11:19 says that Abraham, as he stood above Isaac at the altar, ready to plunge the knife into him, expected God to raise Isaac from the dead. Although he didn't guess exactly how God would be faithful, he never seemed to doubt that He *would* be faithful. And God didn't let him down. The person who genuinely trusts God can be trusted because God can be trusted.

CONSISTENT LIVING

To be trusted, you must consistently behave in a manner that's worthy of trust. As you've grown, your parents (whether they've been aware of it or not) have continually evaluated whether you were trustworthy or not. By now, they know to what extent they can trust you. If you've developed negative patterns of behavior, there's no point in complaining that your parents don't trust you. Actually, they do trust you – they trust you to continue to behave in the ways you've already shown them you tend to behave. You've seen kids who take every opportunity to get into trouble. They sneak, hide, lie, and deceive. Anyone would be a fool to trust that person until his behavior changes. Likewise, if your own patterns of behavior have been negative, the only solution is for you to build trust from scratch.

If that's the case, you should understand right now that building trust takes a long time (which is all the more reason to take special care to maintain it if you already have your parents' trust). To start, you must find ways to be put in responsible situations (small ones, at first) and then behave in a way your parents will approve of. Trust isn't established just by saying, "Mom and Dad – trust me!" You can expect to have to prove yourself in a hundred little ways before you'll be trusted with bigger things.

For example, your parents may look at the rats breeding in the overflowing garbage you were supposed to empty last month and, in response to your request to go on a weekend outing with some friends, say, "If you can't be trusted to empty the garbage, how can you be trusted on an unsupervised weekend?" Sound unfair to you? It isn't – it's perfectly fair. But remember that you can use the same principle to rebuild trust once it has been torn down. Ask your parents what areas they're willing to trust you in, and then work to prove that you're indeed trustworthy in that area. When you've regained their confidence in that area, ask to be trusted in another.

When you've lost your parents' trust, it's easy to convince yourself that it's hopeless to even *try* to rebuild it. It is difficult – but it isn't hopeless. If you really want your parents to regain the faith they once had in you, commit yourself to rebuilding their trust – one step at a time.

The trust Abraham and Isaac demonstrated in each other didn't just happen overnight. They had trusted each other in many little things throughout the years. It's likely that when the camels tore apart Sarah's garden, Abraham showed his godliness just as he did when God presented him with the bigger tests of his faith. The same must have been true with Isaac. Abraham observed Isaac's faith as he grew. He had seen the light in his eyes when he told him of God's promise. He had observed his consistent obedience – and now, when it counted, he fully trusted his son. It is your consistently responsible attention to the little things that will help build your parents' trust for the bigger areas you really care about.

ABSOLUTE HONESTY

Do you want to be trusted? Always tell the truth.

When you lie, regardless of how clever you are, you'll be found out. Your parents may never know the details of your deception, but they will know they are being deceived. Most parents will forgive and forget an admitted mistake or confessed disobedience long before they will forgive an outright lie. And I don't mean just *telling* an untruth. It's also a lie to live in deceit. If you've been secretly disobeying your parents, you're living a lie. If you sincerely want to gain your parents' trust, live your life openly. That means being willing to confess your failures. Your parents know you well enough to know you're not perfect. Hiding your failures doesn't convince them you have none – it simply implies you don't trust them enough to believe they will accept you as you are. It doesn't destroy a parent's confidence to hear you admit to failure. On the contrary, it gives your parents the opportunity to see your growth. They'll be much more inclined to trust you than if you lie by hiding the truth, and they won't find it necessary to second-guess what you're doing. When you admit to doing wrong, you may not avoid punishment – but you will avoid mistrust.

It has been a long time since my children have lied to me. I know that because there have been many admitted mistakes and confessions of disobedience. They don't wait for me to discover their disobedience; they're quick to admit where they've failed. As a result, I trust them.

Lying has a devastating effect on a relationship. When Traci was about five years old, I came out of the bedroom just in time to

see her accidentally drop a jar of buttons on the floor. But she didn't *know* I'd seen it. As she stood staring at the scattered buttons I asked, "What happened?"

I expected her to simply ask for help in cleaning up the mess. Instead, at the sound of my voice, she jerked around in surprise and said, "I didn't do it!" It was such a blatant lie I thought she was kidding. I told her that I'd seen her drop the jar and that it was okay. She persisted with the lie. "I didn't do it, Daddy!" she cried as tears welled up in her eyes.

Her performance was so pathetic and convincing that I found myself wanting to believe her. I was even willing to momentarily doubt what I had just seen with my own eyes. I tried to give her a way out. I begged her. "Please don't lie to me, Traci. I don't intend to punish you, so tell me the truth."

But now she was trapped. Lying is like sticking yourself with a barbed spear. Every second you allow a lie to continue, the spear is driven deeper into your body, and it becomes more painful and damaging to pull it out. With tears streaming down her face and her arms wrapped tightly about me, she sobbed, "Daddy, I would never lie to you. I didn't break the jar."

My understanding was replaced with sadness and anger. I can't tell you how deeply it hurt to have this child I so dearly loved use that love to deceive me. I felt that she could never be trusted. I felt betrayed and alone. I sent her to her room until she could find the courage to tell me the truth.

Because of the lie, a simple matter was now incredibly complicated. If, when I'd first asked, "What happened?" she had simply answered, "I dropped the button jar," it would have been over. We would have picked up the pieces and found a new jar to hold the buttons. Even if I had decided to punish her, no punishment I could have delivered would have equaled the pain and agony spawned by the lie.

After several hours in her room, Traci confessed. But now even her confession left me with doubts: Was she just confessing to get out of her room, or did she really feel sorry? I wasn't sure of anything anymore. That's what lying does.

The next day, my waterbed sprang a leak. I had to throw the whole mattress outside and replace it with a new one. Outside, I refilled the old one with water and told the girls they could invite their friends over to play on it. It was like playing in a bowl of Jello. They had a great time jumping on this blob of fun until I called them for dinner.

As they came through the door I suggested that after dinner they should wet the old mattress down so that it would be slippery as well as bouncy. "Great idea, Daddy," Traci said, and came in to eat.

But when I stepped outside immediately after dinner, I noticed that the mattress was already drenched with water. "You already wet it down, Traci," I said. "You're smarter than me in finding fun ways to use an old waterbed."

With a startled look and big, innocent eyes she said, "Dad – I didn't wet it down."

I couldn't believe my ears. This time I was not going to suffer through all the tears and fake expressions of love. I sent her straight to her room and collapsed into a chair, totally frustrated. Why would she lie about such a trivial thing? I feared that these were the first signs of a crumbling relationship. I could see myself in later years looking back at this moment as the time we began to drift apart. I was heartbroken. I felt completely helpless – but I loved her so much I was not going to give up this easily. I went to her room determined to get the truth. With the same sincere sobs she had used on me the day before, she insisted that she was telling the truth.

I stormed from her room to discuss this further with my wife, Diane, who was just as crushed as I was. As I passed the living-room window, I saw something that stopped me cold: The little neighbor girl was busily watering the waterbed. *Please, God, let this kid be the one who did it,* I prayed as I ran outside. Not only did this imp gleefully admit to dousing the mattress while we were eating dinner, she informed me that she had also washed off our cat and dog.

While I was greatly relieved to discover that Traci hadn't been lying, I also felt guilty for falsely accusing her, and I rushed to her room to ask for forgiveness. It was easy, then, with that experience still fresh in our minds, to explain to her why I hate lying so much. I hate it because it destroys trust.

I told Traci what I will tell you. If you can look your parents in the face and lie, you steal from them the ability to know when you're telling the truth. When Traci looked at me with those big eyes and said she had not wet down that mattress, all I could remember was seeing the same look the day before.

I told Traci what I know your parents would like to tell you. I want to believe everything she says. I don't want to have to guess whether she's telling the truth. I told her that the only possible way for me to trust her so completely again would be for her to promise to never lie. If we could establish that kind of trust, I would believe her even if all the evidence was against her.

With one exception – which she quickly confessed before I even discovered it – she has not lied to me since. If you were to accuse her of murder and had pictures of her standing over the body with a bloody knife in her hand, I would simply take her aside and ask, "Traci, did you do it?" If she said no, I would believe her no matter what the evidence.

Your parents do not find joy in mistrusting you. They want desperately to trust your every word. By refusing to lie, you can make that possible.

CONSTANT COMMUNICATION

Communication builds trust. It keeps you from being misunderstood. If your curfew is at eleven o'clock and you realize that you're going to be late, don't wait until you get home forty-five minutes later to explain what happened. Find a phone and call. Rather than trying to explain the situation to half-crazed parents who have spent forty-five minutes thinking of all the ways you could be dead, you'll be talking to fairly rational human beings.

Because you had the courtesy to call, they'll be willing to trust you in the future.

Of course, once you understand this principle, you might be tempted to use it in a manipulative way to get to stay out late and often. Don't give in to that temptation. It works only in emergencies, and even then it will be questioned if it's used too often. If you start putting your parents up against the wall by constantly calling to say you're going to be late, they'll quickly catch on to your scam.

When you say you're going to be someplace, be there. If you change your mind, call and let them know where you are going to be instead. Seem like a lot of unnecessary work? Consider the problem it avoids. Suppose you tell your parents you're going to the pizza shop and end up going to the mall instead. If your parents try to call you at the pizza shop, and the manager tells them you're not there, they have to believe one of three things: that you're hurt, that you lied, or that you changed your mind and didn't call to let them know. If you've lied in the recent past, they'll assume that you lied – they won't *want* to assume that, but the evidence will point toward it. If not, the Worry Gremlin will be showing them how you died.

A trusting relationship should include the courtesy of letting your parents know where you are. A trusting parent would only call for a very important reason. If you're not where you said you would be, no matter how much you're trusted, they'll be upset. It only takes a moment to call. That moment can save you hours of hassle if they ever need to reach you.

CONSTANT VIGILANCE

The secret to maintaining trust is really no secret: it's consistency. You must *consistently* follow the patterns outlined above. If you can only be trusted sometimes, then you can't be trusted. Years of building trust can come crashing down around you with a single betrayal. And when that happens, it can take you a long

149   **Building on The Big "T"**

time to rebuild that trust.

After a program I did on this subject, a young lady approached me with the following story. Her parents had left her in charge of their home for a few days while they went away on business. She had begged her parents for this responsibility and convinced them she could be trusted. They laid down a few ground rules, including the stipulation that she would not entertain any of her friends in the home while they were gone. She obeyed that rule – with one exception. Shortly after her parents left, her boyfriend invited himself over for the evening. He pressured her into spending several nights together.

This girl's parents called on several occasions. She felt bad about lying to them as her boyfriend sat right there in the same room. The parents concluded their business early and came home to discover their daughter in bed with her boyfriend.

A relationship of mutual trust that had taken many years to build was destroyed in an instant. The fact that the boyfriend had exerted considerable pressure on the girl didn't matter. The fact that the girl had felt crushing guilt didn't matter. What did matter was that she had broken her promise.

When she spoke to me that evening, she was hurting as badly as I have seen a teenager hurt. She said, "Ken, it has been over a month since that happened, and my parents still don't trust me."

I reminded her that broken trust can't be rebuilt in a month. It could take years. Sometimes it can never be rebuilt. That's why the trust you build with your parents must be carefully protected. Once it's destroyed, you start all over. Demonstrating consistent responsibility and trustworthy behavior is the only way to maintain trust. If you consider betraying your parents' trust, you had better carefully weigh the benefits of whatever you're thinking of doing against the priceless value of being trusted.

In conclusion, trust is the most important aspect of any relationship. It's at the core of our relationship with Christ. You can be the catalyst to establishing trust in your family. Begin by strengthening your faith in God. Then reread this chapter and implement in your life the steps that will bring trust to your home.

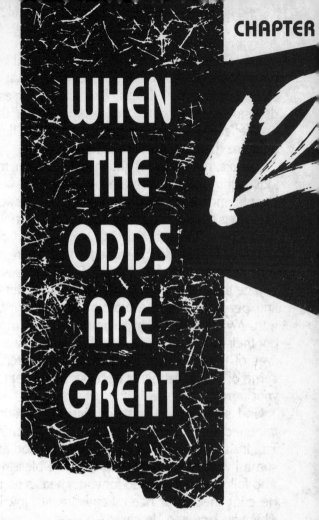

WHEN THE ODDS ARE GREAT

Some of you reading this book will feel greatly discouraged because you believe your family is different. If your parents fight all the time, or are divorced, or aren't Christians, you may be tempted to say, "This stuff is okay for normal families, but it wouldn't work for me." If you're facing a family crisis, or if one of your parents has died, or if you're living with other people than your parents, you might assume that the information in this book doesn't apply to you.

Not so. These principles work whether you have a model family or not. There are very few model families. All families struggle and have problems. Many teenagers come from single-parent families. Many families face illness, financial struggles, alcoholism, drug dependency, and other major problems. If the love of Christ is only effective in perfect homes, then His love means nothing, because there are no perfect homes.

You are not alone. Right this minute, there are thousands of kids facing the problems that you thought were unique to you. I want to encourage you to believe that the power and love of Jesus Christ has transformed lives in the most horrible of circumstances, from concentration camps to war zones. No matter what your situation, He can do the same for you. There is no guarantee that your problems will go away, but God promises that you don't have to face those problems alone. With the power of His love you can find peace and have a profound impact on the people you live with. My files are full of testimonies from moms and dads who got their lives straightened out because they saw God's love in the lives of their children. This chapter is written to help you make some of the adjustments necessary to meet the special needs of your family.

God sent Jesus Christ for sinners – for imperfect people in imperfect families. He healed the sick and ministered to the poor. The instructions written in the Word of God are for *you* – not for some hypothetical perfect family. The blessings that await those who follow Christ are also for you. There is no problem so big that He can't meet your need. Read on with joy, because He knows what you face and He cares.

WHAT IF MY PARENTS AREN'T CHRISTIANS?

If your parents have never trusted Christ for the forgiveness of their sins, you're faced with a double dilemma. First, you want them to understand your beliefs; second, you want them to experience the same forgiveness and joy you have. On both counts, the key is clear communication of your faith and a disciplined life that demonstrates that faith.

I know many Christian teenagers who live fairly clean lives but don't demonstrate their faith at home. They would never consider taking a drink or smoking a joint because of what it would do to their testimony. But they treat their families like the lowest forms of life on earth. The greatest witness you will have to your parents is the way you live at home. Your willingness to forgive, your desire to be obedient, and your efforts to love your family will carry more weight than all the preaching in the world.

But don't forget: It's also important to communicate the basics of your faith and how you want that faith to affect your life. If you've never communicated your faith to your parents, let me suggest a way. First, arrange for a time to talk with them. You may want to take them to dinner or some quiet, nonthreatening place where you won't be interrupted by nuisances such as the phone. Explain that you want them to understand the most important thing in your life – then, briefly and simply, explain your commitment to Christ. Don't preach; simply share what He means to you and express your desire to show His love in the way you live at home. Ask your parents to be patient with you when you fail, and to also kindly remind you of areas that need improvement. This kind of vulnerability reduces the risk of sounding "holier than thou." Let them know that, because of the joy and forgiveness that Christ has brought to you, you would love nothing more than to someday have them know Him too. Then tell your parents how much you love them. Ask them to help you in your efforts to live for Christ and give them a chance to ask questions.

This shouldn't be a professional speech, but rather a well-thought-out, heart-to-heart talk. If you're scared, tell them so. If you wish you had done this long ago, let them know that. If you're afraid you'll let them down, tell them. Most parents long for such open communication from their children. They may not immediately decide to become Christians, but they won't forget what you've said. That information will become the focal point of the changes they see in your life. They will know why those changes are taking place.

The greatest risk you face is that they will bring this up again at some time when you're really blowing it. But look at it this way: That isn't really a risk! Instead, it's your greatest motivation to keep on striving to improve. When you make a mistake, apologize and allow them to see that you're truly sorry – and by "truly sorry" I mean sorry because you realize you have done wrong, not sorry because you were caught. Don't be defensive about the fact that you blew it. Your parents will appreciate your openness and ready attitude to try to do better. Then move forward. Although it may seem that they expect you to be perfect, they don't. They know you aren't perfect because they live with you. But they will be watching to see how Christianity works for imperfect people. Why? Because they know that *they* are imperfect, and if it works for you they may conclude that it will also work for them.

WHEN YOUR PARENTS ARE WRONG

It's always difficult to be right when the people who have authority over you are wrong. A parent's authority makes it much easier for him to say, "You're wrong!" But what if your parents are wrong? Do you ignore the problem because you have no power to change it? Or do you risk the problems that can come with confronting someone who is in authority over you? Confrontation – especially that kind – isn't easy, and the risks of being misunderstood are high. Here are some suggestions:

1. Be careful about making any judgments. It's easy to misjudge your parents and falsely accuse them of being wrong. More than one teenager who has made that accusation has, after carefully reconsidering the situation and letting some time go by, realized that his parents had been right all along. Weigh the evidence well before you jump to conclusions.

2. Give them the right to be wrong. Teenagers often expect perfection from their parents. Your parents are no different from you. They struggle to do right and sometimes fall flat on their faces. Parents are tempted; they sin; they even make stupid mistakes. (There's only one exception to that, and I'm the exception.) It's easy to so idealize your parents that you can't forgive them for the same weaknesses you have. Give them a break. If your mother and father struggle with sin, then love and forgive them. That attitude will allow you to approach them with understanding love when you confront them.

3. Don't try to confront in the midst of emotion. Wait until both you and your parents have cool heads before you try to express your concerns. If you confront them during emotional peaks, any of you might say things that should never be spoken. Wait until you're calm.

4. Avoid accusation. You'll get much further if you talk about how their behavior makes you feel, rather that blatantly accusing your parents of wrong.

A boy from Denver lived with the worsening alcoholism of his father for years before he finally talked with him about it. On the way to a basketball game, he told his dad how deeply it hurt to see him ruining his life. His father bluntly responded that it was none of the boy's business what he did with his life. For many teenagers that would have been the end of the conversation. This boy, with wisdom beyond his years, replied, "Dad, I love you. That makes it my business."

I would love to report that the conversation was the turning point in this father's life and that he never touched a drop of booze again. That's not the case. But that father and son never made it to the basketball game – they spent that evening in a truck stop, opening up to each other as they had not done for years. Now, the father no longer struggles alone, and the son understands his father more than ever before. If the son had responded to his father's first rude reply with accusations, the communication would have ended on the spot.

There are risks that come with saying to your mother and father, "I think your actions are wrong, and they hurt me deeply." Parents aren't always willing to admit that they're wrong, nor are they always willing to accept your point of view. But the damage that results

155

from holding those feelings inside and allowing them to fester far outweighs the risks involved with loving confrontation.

During a visit to my parents' home I was confronted by my ten-year-old daughter. The problem was that, when visiting my parents, I often would allow my language to become vulgar and crude, maybe in an attempt to express my adulthood to parents who had been very strict when I was young. Regardless of the reason, the language was inappropriate and didn't go unnoticed by Traci.

While she was preparing for bed one evening, she began to cry. It took me a long time to get her to talk about what was causing her sadness. When she finally did speak, her words cut to my very soul. She didn't imply that I was a terrible person or accuse me of having a dirty mouth. Instead, she told me how my talk confused and hurt her. I tried to justify my actions with several good excuses, but the more I talked the more I realized that she was right and I was *so* wrong. I made a promise to be more careful with my tongue, and I asked her to help me.

I can honestly say that her confrontation that night has changed the way I talk. She made me aware that many people were watching my life, expecting to see consistency in my behavior. Her confrontation wasn't an insult. It was the expression of a girl who respected her father and was disappointed by his behavior. She wanted me to be a first-class dad wherever I was. She was right, and that's just what I want to be.

WHEN THERE IS CRISIS IN THE FAMILY

Crisis puts an extra load of stress on a family that can draw them closer together or blow them apart. Divorce, illness, death, and a host of other devastating events can test the bonds that hold a family together. Each time your family goes through a crisis, the psychological complexity of that experience could fill a book – and, in each of those books, your ability to cope would

When The Odds Are Great

always come back to your attitude. Are you willing to consider the needs of the other members of the family above your own? Are you willing to pitch in and provide some of the teamwork needed to bring a family through rough times? Families that draw closer during a crisis do so because the crisis helps them realize how much they need each other.

While a friend of mine was recovering from a heart attack, his wife asked me to come to their home. In this time of crisis, one of their daughters was being very difficult. That, added to the uncertainty of her husband's health, had brought this mom to the breaking point.

I went upstairs and briefly tried to help the daughter understand the unbelievable pressures her mom was facing. I told her that, if ever her mom needed her love and cooperation, it was now. She came downstairs and talked with her mother. It was a turning point. Later, that mother said that they had learned to say, "I'm sorry." I did nothing magical or unique; it was their realization of how much they needed each other that made the difference. By being willing to apologize and help each other through this crisis, they relieved some of the tensions that could only have added to the problem.

Does it sound as if I'm suggesting that, if we just pray and be good, everything will be better? It doesn't always work that way – sometimes help must come from outside the family. If the problems you're facing seem overwhelming, it's important that you seek help from a competent Christian counselor. Your pastor or youth pastor can be an excellent source of help during difficult times. If they feel unable to help you, they can refer you to someone who can.

Needing counseling isn't something to be ashamed of. It's not a sign of weakness; it's a sign of maturity and strength. Throughout the Bible, we are encouraged to seek counsel from wise men and women that love the Lord. In very difficult home situations, family counseling provides an outside view that sometimes brings a clearer perspective to both parties.

When there is physical or sexual abuse, it is absolutely necessary that you get outside help immediately. And if you don't get help from the first person you talk with, keep trying until you do. Many abused children are afraid to tell anyone about how they're being treated because of the terrible problems that will result when people find out. As good counselors will tell you, it *will* be very difficult at first – but the long-term effects of continued abuse far outweigh the initial pain of telling someone. Don't give up until you get help.

Don't wait for a crisis before calling on the Lord. Instead, start now to build a faith in God that you can draw on when times are rough. You don't wait until you're on a sinking ship to learn to swim. Remember Abraham? He didn't come by his faith overnight. When the big test came, he was ready – because he had built a reservoir of faith by trusting God with little things over a long period of time.

If you find yourself facing crisis now without that reservoir of faith, don't despair. Your simple faith in God to face the moments of helplessness will be met with the strength to take it one step at a time. He promises, in 1 Corinthians 10:13, that we will not be tempted beyond what we can bear: "No temptation has seized you except what is common to man. And God is faithful; he will not let you be tempted beyond what you can bear. But when you are tempted, he will also provide a way out so that you can stand up under it."

During these times, don't hesitate to express your need for support from other members of the family. You'll be helping them as well as getting support for yourself. Helping someone else in the midst of crisis is one of the best ways to get your eyes off your own problems. When you request the help of other members of your family, you give them the opportunity to give.

No problem is too big for you and the Lord. Romans 8:38-39 says, "For I am convinced that neither death nor life, neither angels nor demons, neither the present nor the future, nor any powers, neither height nor depth, nor anything else in all creation, will be able to separate us from the love of God that is in Christ Jesus our Lord."

When The Odds Are Great

Philippians 4:13: "I can do everything through him who gives me strength."

You're no different from David, Abraham, Paul, or any of the other Bible heroes who faced difficult odds. With Christ, you can be victorious.